Play and Learn in the Early Years

Jennie Lindon, Kevin Kelman and Alice Sharp

CONTENTS

Published by Step Forward Publishing Limited
St Jude's Church, Dulwich Road, Herne Hill, London, SE24 0PB Tel. 020 7738 5454
www.practicalpreschool.com

A time of learning

Babies and toddlers are primed to learn and recent research into the development of the human brain has shown the significance of appropriate early experiences. Realistic expectations, based on reliable information about development, are crucial for good early years practice. It is important that you do not expect too much, too soon – but also that you do not underestimate the skills and understanding of very young children. The difference between a young baby and a three year old is visible and striking. However, by three years of age it is also possible to see the differences between young children who have had happy and interesting early years and those who are already uncertain about their abilities and how adults will treat them.

What is happening around young children?

Babies and young children have not changed at all. However, some parts of the UK have now issued guidance about the care and learning needs of babies and very young children, when they attend registered early years provision of any kind.

Up to 2002 any national early childhood guidance across the UK was focussed on the over threes. In the autumn of that year the Birth to Three Matters framework was introduced in England and in 2005 Scotland launched their Birth to Three: Supporting our Youngest Children. The English and Scottish under threes materials looked different but the principles and practical applications were very similar.

The most recent change (at the time of writing) is that from September 2008 in England the Birth to Three Matters framework and the Curriculum Guidance for the Foundation Stage (applying to three-, four- and five-year-olds) will both be replaced by the Early Years Foundation Stage. The EYFS covers the full early childhood from birth to five years. Practitioners will recognise a great deal of the content of Birth to Three Matters within the EYFS materials.

A positive outlook on very young children

Under threes deserve our respect just as much as our attentive care. The following key principles underpin all the suggestions in this book. They are fully compatible with those expressed in national guidance.

Under threes are interesting in their own right

You need to focus on individual babies and toddlers as they are in the present, rather than on developmental stages or milestones that are weeks or months into the future. A sound knowledge of child development does matter, but also a firm grasp of the holistic, connected nature of young learning. Babies and very young children do not learn in separate categories. Within any experience or activity, young skills and enthusiasm will always embrace more than one aspect or area of learning.

- Appreciate babies and toddlers as they are now: what they can manage and what they can nearly do, what they find fascinating and the ways in which they relate to the world. What they are learning is important for itself and not just for what will happen later.
- If you are alert to all the exciting smaller changes and learning, an individual baby or young child will learn more easily. Also, your day will be more interesting and satisfying.
- **Get into the habit of 'baby watching' and notice what individual babies and toddlers do and how they do it. Keep notes as appropriate and take photos. (You will have cleared this option with parents when their child joins your provision.) Then you can share your observations with parents and you can all look back with interest.**

Care and caring matter

Emotional security is a non-negotiable priority for babies and very young children. Early learning cannot be supported if personal care is undervalued - if very young children cannot count on a nurturing environment. Young children did not create the artificial division between 'care' and 'education' that remains a problem within early years services.

- Nurture matters a very great deal to young children. They appreciate and are warmed by personal and respectful attention to their physical needs.
- Babies and toddlers will learn better in an environment where care genuinely matters and is never seen as somehow second best to 'educational' activities, however those are defined.
- Personal care routines are valuable times for warm communication and developing a close relationship between baby and carer.
- Very young children learn when they are welcomed as active helpers in simple domestic routines.

Young children deserve generous time and attention

Admittedly, some days can seem very full and busy. But it is possible to become more harassed than necessary by losing your perspective on how very young children learn.

- The early years are indeed a window of opportunity, but only if caring adults go at the baby's pace and in tune with a child's interests.
- Children switch off learning if they are pressurised and constantly directed by what adults think they ought to be learning now.
- You and the children have time: to relish experiences, to do interesting activities again, to stop and look and just to be together.

Flexible planning rests on a child-friendly rhythm to the day

It is useful to have some plans for each day and young children like a sense of routine.

- You need to look at a baby's or toddler's day as a whole and not as a list of separate activities. By all means plan ahead for possibilities over a week and the separate days. But then go with the flow of what interests the children each day. Be ready to pause, change direction and to follow a child's lead.
- Look towards what works well in family life. Home-based learning is the developmentally appropriate model for very young children – and that approach should not stop at three years. There is serious concern about over threes who are pushed into formal and very adult-controlled days.
- Young children relish a blend of novelty and familiarity. They enjoy new experiences, but they also learn from recognising a play activity or local outing. Sometimes the best choice for learning is 'let's do it again!'

Enjoy – there is no obligation always to make something. Older babies and toddlers like hands-on activities, such as play dough, simple sticking and drawing.

- Enjoy the activity with the toddlers and do not be concerned whether something emerges that can be used as a display. Enjoyable learning will often leave a happy memory, rather than an end product like a picture or model.
- Share with parents how much the children enjoyed the finger painting or how they have learned to use a thick crayon.
- Be careful not to push very young children into making something just because you feel a pressure to show an item to parents at the end of the day.

Caring adults count more than equipment

Think of yourself as the most vital item of play equipment in your nursery or home setting.

- If you relate warmly to babies and toddlers, they will learn supported within that relationship. On the other hand, when adults are uninvolved or uninterested in babies and toddlers, then good play equipment cannot make up that loss.
- Try to see the world through their eyes and hear with their ears. They have so much to learn and what is obvious to you may be intriguing or puzzling to them.
- Be close to very young children and at their eye level. Make it easy for them to engage with you.
- Be enthusiastic about activities with the children, be a part of what they do. If you are genuinely interested, children are more likely to learn.

Balance safety with interest and opportunity for adventure

Babies and toddlers have no sense of danger and their natural curiosity can lead them into trouble.

- They need your keen eye for their safety. But look for ways to meet their curiosity rather than limit them to a safe but boring world.
- If you are closely engaged with them, you can keep very young children safe by gentle intervention that does not disrupt their play.
- Any setting should remove obvious hazards and avoid the preventable accidents. However, babies and toddlers will not be able to learn if adults are so concerned about a long list of what could go wrong that they remove anything of interest.

Important note:
All the ideas within this book assume that adults will be attentive and closely involved in the play of very young children. None are intended as something you set out and then leave for young children to do on their own. Our assumption is that a caring and interested adult will always be close to babies and toddlers. Although some suggestions have additional safety reminders, this general comment applies to everything that follows.

How to use this book

The book is organised into three main age sections:

- Under twelve months – the babies
- From one to two years of age – the toddlers
- From two to three years of age – very young children.

We are aware that the English EYFS has a series of overlapping age spans. We found it more workable to stay with one year of life. Some older babies will be ready for a few of the toddler activities. Three- or even four-year-olds will still enjoy some ideas first introduced for younger children. You can also choose ideas to fit the developmental stage of children, whose early experience or disability means that they will benefit from a range of play activities more usually offered to younger children.

There are five broad theme areas that are repeated within each age section:

- Developing relationships: early communication and social life;
- Using the senses: vision, touch, smell and hearing;
- Language and Creative Development: arts and crafts, music and stories;
- Physical Development: large and fine physical skills;
- Using the environment: outdoor play and trips out.

The aim is that you use this material as a resource, to draw on and re-organise as suits the children and your setting. It is not intended that you treat any section as an inflexible programme to be done with the children from beginning to end.

From birth to twelve months

Development within the first year

Babies learn within affectionate and close relationships with a small number of carers, including their parents, who take the time to know this very young person as an individual. Young babies do sleep for many hours in total, but that still leaves waking times in which they enjoy company and increasingly want to be entertained. Some babies have long wakeful periods from the early months and carers need a range of ideas and the willingness to chat with and carry around babies who simply do not want to be left alone.

Babies' interests and skills will build towards the more recognisable milestones, such as the 'first word' or 'first steps', so long as you value all the finer developments on the way. The first gestures and meaningful looks are forms of early communication and vital if recognisable words are to emerge later. A great deal of exciting physical movement and practice happens long before the first tottering steps. You will find life far more interesting with babies if you are attuned to what is happening day by day.

Learning to control their own limbs and whole body is a major focus for babies. Watch how much effort they put into the fine and larger movements and how hard they will try again and again to grab that interesting rattle or to get moving as a crawler. Mobility is a big issue, from the perspective of a baby. Once gained, confident mobility opens up a whole new world. Even being able to sit without falling over, means that the baby has her hands free to play and explore.

Babies need a great deal of physical care for their health, growth and well being. However, physical caring also contributes to vital, close relationships between baby and carer and to the baby's sense of self worth when she is treated with patience and respect. Caring routines can and should be social times and opportunities for baby and carer to get to know each other better. There is no 'just' about care and caring from the baby's perspective!

Babies do not make any distinction between learning and playing. They learn through what engages their interest and are supported by caring adults, whom they trust. Once you acknowledge that babies can learn through everything in which they participate, there will be no need to create special 'educational' activities. Babies and young children learn a great deal through happy involvement in the normal routines of their day and such events have meaning for them.

Developing relationships

Early communication

Developmental focus

Babies communicate from their earliest weeks, many months before their first recognisable words. Their crying becomes more varied and they make sounds that reflect their mood. Babies' increasing control of their mouth, tongue and lips means that they become able to make an ever wider range of sounds. By five to six months they are making strings of sounds. They smile and chuckle to engage your attention and for sheer pleasure. Between about six and twelve months, babies become adept at communicating with a range of vocalisations through sound making. They also use the full support of their facial expression and useful gestures like pointing, to direct your attention and share their current interests.

Babies need to be able to hear clear words, in a meaningful context before they will start to understand and use words spontaneously. Attentive adults are the very best source of support to encourage babies to communicate. They need real people to respond with interest and enthusiasm to all their early efforts. Electronic consoles or cuddly toys with a battery-driven 'voice' do not help a baby (or toddler) to learn to listen and speak. However sophisticated the technology, no toy can know which words are of interest to this older baby or young toddler.

Let's have a chat

- Babies and young children have to be able to hear you, to distinguish sounds, and then words, easily. So cut down on unnecessary background noise and avoid bad habits of raising your voice regularly or shouting.
- It does not matter exactly what you say to babies so long as you sound interesting and interested in their response. Research suggests that it does matter how you talk with babies – a modified form of communication called infant-directed speech.
- The trick is to talk in a more expressive way than you might to older children or adults. Repeat yourself in

slightly different words. Talk more slowly than usual and leave pauses for the baby to join the 'conversation'.
- For instance, you might say with a light tone throughout, 'I had a terrible time on the bus this morning (pause and look at the baby). Oh, yes I did. (pause and a smile). That bus would not come (pause). No it wouldn't (pause) and I got so cold waiting. (pause). You're grinning, yes you are (pause and a smile). You don't mind me getting cold (pause). What a one you are (pause and affectionate touch). You just wait until you have to go on the bus, yes, you just wait' and so on in a circling way that engages a baby's interest.

Add the words

- Talk simply about what you are doing in a baby's physical care routines. Use words and short phrases that link directly with what you are doing with or for the baby – for example, 'let's take your hat off' or 'here's your drink'.
- Listen, watch and respond to the baby's sounds, expressions and gestures. Add some words that are appropriate to the situation.
- If she stretches out a hand towards the teddy, you say, 'do you want the teddy?' as you hand it over. If her eyes swivel round at the sound of someone entering the room, say, 'look, it's Marsha. Shall we say "Hello" to Marsha?'

Ooh look!

- Within the second half of the first year, babies start to point: a very useful social skill to engage your attention and share their interests and wishes.
- Show babies that you are interested in what catches their attention.
- Add your simple comments about what the baby can directly experience through her senses.
- Follow her excited point with, 'oh, yes, look. It's our robin back again'. Show delight in the tinkling made by her rattle with, 'listen, you made it work. Can I have a go?'
- Respond to what the baby notices close by with comments like, 'yes, Jamal's crying, isn't he' or 'that's right, there's our lunch coming in. Are you hungry? I am.'

Play and chat

- Babies are intrigued by people or toys who temporarily disappear. Play peep-bo by moving in and out of the baby's vision – not too fast . Say, 'Hello! as you reappear.
- Cover your head with a cloth or scarf that you or the baby pulls off. If the baby wants, let her cover her head. Say, 'where's Sally? Where's she gone?' and then, 'there you are!'. Toddlers still love this game and may like you to cover their whole body.
- Follow the baby's lead when something she enjoys doing can turn into a game to be shared. It might be making a funny face with the lips puckered up, blowing raspberries, pointing and chuckling or putting her hand on the page of a book so you cannot turn it over. Add suitable words to the game, such as, 'what a face that is!' or 'can't I turn the page then? No?'
- Babies like games when you or the baby gives something and takes it back, perhaps many times. Add words like, 'is this for me?' and 'oh, you want it back. I thought it was mine', accompanied by smiles.

Pause for thought

Warm communication with babies is the bedrock of the close and affectionate relationship that is necessary for them to thrive. This central principle is emphasised in the Scottish Birth to Three by being one of the three Rs – Relationships, with Responsiveness and Respect. In the English EYFS one of the four themes underpinning good practice is that of Positive Relationships.

Young children need to form strong and enduring bonds of affection within their own family. But they also need to feel welcomed and cherished by their out-of-home carers. The security and trust that evolves with these attachments builds the basis for later social development.

Social life

Developmental focus

Babies are primed and ready to become social beings. They stare intently at human faces and strive for close physical contact. They want the reassuring sounds and scents of another human body, soon to become familiar to them. Babies, and toddlers, need to develop an affectionate relationship with their childminder and to their key person in a nursery setting.

Supportive early years practitioners take time to reassure parents that babies can and do form attachments to more than one person. You let parents know when babies missed them or were happy to see them come back in at the end of the day. Partnership with families ensures that parents feel confident that you welcome hearing about their time at home with the baby.

Just the two of us

- Babies will learn later about being part of a social group because they have been treated as an individual now. So look for any preferences that this baby shows about how she likes to be treated.
- Greet babies when they wake or when you first see them today as a carer. Let them know that you notice they are here, when they have woken from sleep and when they leave to go home. Babies and young children should feel confident that they have a secure place in your memory; you keep them in mind.
- Notice whether a baby shows special interest in one song rather than another. Does she like to be taken to stare at this particular picture or wall poster? Does one baby like a game in which you wiggle her toes but another baby likes to be bounced gently on your lap.
- Use the valuable close time of physical care to look at babies and to communicate with them. Find a personal ritual that is slightly different for each baby in your care. Perhaps it is a special funny face you make or a rhyme that particularly makes this baby smile.

Help babies to make contact

- Make it easy for slightly older babies (about four to twelve months) to watch what is going on as well as to explore their own suitable play materials. Make sure that their baby seat is placed so that they can watch you or other children.

- Provide a safe base for babies to watch. Sit on the floor and have babies on your lap, sitting within your crossed legs or let them lean against your body.
- Watch as babies crawl off or toddle away to explore. Wave to them and greet them with, 'You're back!' as they return.
- By seven to eight months, babies can sit safely and their hands are free to enjoy the contents of a treasure basket (see page 8). Two babies sitting at the basket will enjoy watching the other one and may start to offer items to each other.
- Take a moment to watch when older babies are trying to make contact. They use pats and prods that may sometimes unintentionally hurt a bit. If necessary, show babies how to be more gentle in their body clasps and soften a firm grip on someone's hair or ear (it may be yours).
- Babies are interested in other babies and slightly older children so long as they are not rushed or required to be friendly to unfamiliar people. Care in a family home can bring contact with older children; look for ways in a nursery to bring the age groups together for at least some of the day.

All a game

- Babies like to play repetitive games in which they have a role different from that of the adult or older child. Be patient and play the same game as often as the baby enjoys.
- Play social games when the baby gives you a toy and then immediately takes it back again or when they drop or throw a toy that you fetch. Join in the fun with warm remarks like 'But I thought that was for me!' or 'Ooh, how many more times?'
- Look for games that this baby develops and respond with enjoyment. One baby might relish holding down the page of the board book just as you are about to turn it. Another baby might love pointing to parts of the room and getting you to look. Yet another baby might most enjoy it when you copy her sound making.
- Babies are often enchanted by the attention of older children. The slightly older boys and girls are often adept at entertaining younger ones with the kind of repetitive games and sound plays that babies love.

Using the senses

Helping babies to look and enjoy

Developmental focus

Eye contact plays an important role in the initial stages of the first close attachment to parents and other key carers involved with young babies. They need time and the welcome to gaze at you, sometimes with a penetrating stare. Babies explore their world actively with their eyes. From birth, they turn their heads towards diffuse sources of light, and react to bright light by closing their eyes. During the first weeks, babies focus best on objects 20-30cm from their eyes. An adult carer's face should be naturally at this distance when holding the baby.

When they cannot yet move independently, babies need you to bring them interesting sights or to carry them across to take a good look. Babies are naturally visually curious and their gaze will move over anything of interest, with easy distraction to something else. If you help them to look and learn in the early months, they will begin later to hold their gaze on something intriguing. They will also use their physical skills to explore and to move the object so they can take an even better look.

Look at that!

- Toys and mobiles hanging over a cot at 20-30 cm distance encourage the baby to focus. By around four months, babies start to realise that when they see something they can reach out and touch it.
- Babies' attentions are caught by striking contrasts. It may be a soft toy like a panda or abstract patterns and paintings. They are interested in all kinds of play materials and not just what are sold as 'baby toys'.
- Follow the baby's gaze; what interests her? Be ready to repeat any games that make her smile or look intently. Have plenty of resources to hand for babies' visual interest, but do not overload with too much at any one time. Let a baby stare, enjoy and then move on to gazing at something or someone else.

Pause for thought

Elinor Goldschmied observed the fascination of babies and toddlers with ordinary household objects and developed the idea into a learning resource that she called the Treasure Basket. Anita Hughes worked with her and their concern about there being far too many plastic toys is as current as ever. This idea is very flexible and promotes a broad range of learning for babies and toddlers.

Gather a range of materials that vary in feel and texture and keep them in a low, open basket.

- Collect ordinary, safe objects like small containers, large cotton reels, fir cones, woolly balls, a firm fruit like a lemon, a wooden spoon or spatula, large wooden curtain rings, a bath sponge, a small scoop or pastry cutters, old-fashioned dolly clothes pegs.
- Make a collection that varies in look, texture, shape and smell so that babies can explore in any way they wish.
- Make sure that no object is so small that a baby could swallow it.
- Watch out if you use the resource with older children with learning disabilities. Children may still put objects in their mouth, which will be bigger than a baby's.

The basket is for babies who are able to sit up comfortably, either without any help or with support for their back. Put the basket on the floor, sit one or two babies up to it and watch from close by. Let them play as they wish and do not intervene unless a baby's play is unsafe – to her or another baby. Give babies time to explore the objects however they want. Toddlers often still enjoy the treasure basket and this activity can be extended into other resources.

Look and learn

- Attach safe wooden and plastic utensils, shiny CDs, strips of coloured paper and tissues to a line using bulldog clips. Fix this home-made mobile over the cot or the comfortable area where babies (or toddlers) lie on their backs for a restful quiet time. The items will be even more interesting if they move with a gentle draft of air.
- Try fixing the same range of items onto a hula hoop and suspending the hoop from the ceiling or secure beam with string fixed at several points round the hoop circle.

- Hang a prism in front of the window and on sunny days rainbows will appear on the wall.
- Blow bubbles for the baby to track and perhaps reach for.
- Use bright glove puppets in tracking games. Sing 'Incy Wincy Spider' with a spider puppet.
- Between six and nine months, babies will look for any toy they drop. Partially hide a toy under something and ask the baby to find it (using gestures as well as your words). Eventually, you will be able to hide the item completely when they are watching and they will be able to find it again
- At about the same age most babies will enjoy peek-a-boo. Play the game with them and also let babies look in a mirror to see reflections change as they move.

A rolling book

- For this activity you need empty baby milk tins (check that there are no sharp edges), photographs, magazine pictures, wrapping paper.
- Select pictures of familiar items, such as family members, animals, toys or fruit. Laminate the pictures and then glue or tape the pictures onto the tin.
- Roll the tin for the baby to watch, pointing at and talking about the different pictures. Make comments such as 'Where's the ball?' 'Can you see a face?' Answer your own questions with, 'there it is.'
- As alternatives, use black and white squares on the tin (especially for babies up to two months). Or cover tins with simple patterns in two colours.

Moving lights

- You need a torch and to make sure babies are comfortable, sitting or lying.
- Dull the lights so that the beam of the torch can be seen easily. Put the torch on and move it slowly around the room.
- Watch the baby following it with their eyes. (Never flash the light, as this can be distressing.)
- Extend this activity by cutting basic shapes, such as hearts or diamonds, out of different coloured cellophane or gels. Or place a revolving lamp in the room, at a safe distance from the babies.

Flying saucers

- Draw bold, simple and colourful designs on paper plates: squares, giant polka dots, stripes, stars.
- Hang the plates with ribbon around the baby in the cot or elsewhere in the nursery. Ensure they are always beyond babies' reach when you are not there.

- As alternatives, use paper plates with pre-printed designs, or draw faces on the paper plates. Add wool for hair and make sure they are smiling.

Bring a bottle

- Assemble empty 250ml plastic bottles, coloured water/liquid, bubble bath, scraps of bright materials, glitter, tinsel, fabric conditioner, feathers.
- Fill the bottles with a variety of objects and coloured liquids. Then check the bottle lids are secure.
- Slowly, gently shake one bottle in front of the baby's face. Move it slowly from side to side, then from above the head, then down again.
- Continue with the other bottles and extend this activity by using alternative materials in the bottles such as sequins, glass beads, shelled nuts or holographic paper.

Pause for thought
An array of filled, plastic bottles gives babies and toddlers sustained interest throughout early childhood. This home-made collection is a good example of how a flexible play resource will be enjoyed across a wide age range. Babies enjoy the items when you hold the bottle for them. Older babies and young toddlers seize the bottles independently. Later they happily load up a selection of bottles in their bag or little trolley.

Touch

Developmental focus

Touch is more than a physical skill; it is also an important source of information. Direct physical contact helps babies to learn about their own body and the world around them. Touch is also part of communication. So, making close contact is very important within an affectionate relationship between babies and parents or familiar carers.

In the early weeks, babies grasp a finger placed in their hand. Between one to two months, they begin to find their own hands and experiment by holding one hand with the other and opening and shutting their fingers. By about two months babies start to grasp a toy placed in their hands and soon learn to keep hold and wave the toy about. By about three months, babies can find their hands and play with them deliberately, watching their moving fingers and putting a finger or thumb into their mouth. From three to six months, babies can learn to look, reach out and swipe at or grasp toys. From six to twelve months babies are using a range of physical skills to make contact, hold onto an object and explore it.

Making direct contact

- Very young babies want to feel the physical boundaries to their world. If you bathe young babies hold them so that their feet touch the end of the baby bath. They will be reassured by the contact; anxious babies will be calmed so that they can then enjoy the feel of the water.
- Get wakeful babies' attention with warm words and a gentle touch to their hands, cheek or body. Look and smile. Combine friendly conversation with physical contact, so that babies are encouraged to communicate.
- Tune into what individual babies like. Some enjoy a gentle tickle or walking your fingers up an arm or over their stomach. Touch their hand or stroke their cheek while murmuring friendly words.

Within reach

Help babies develop the combination of look, reach and touch.

2-3 months

- Place a suitable toy into the baby's hands. Talk with the baby about what you are doing. Repeat with the same or other toys for so long as the baby is interested. .
- Provide safe mobiles that a baby can stretch out for and touch or swipe at. Watch and share in the babies' fun when they connect.

4-5 months

- Hold a toy steady and wait patiently for babies to look, touch and grasp. Be pleased with them and perhaps say, 'you've got it!' Repeat with other items that interest them.

Touch and explore

- Collect play materials for babies to shake, watch and create a sound. As well as bought sound-making toys, make shakers from see-through plastic bottles (with a firm lid) and add orange lentils, coloured pasta shapes, shiny beads or sequins.
- Offer toys to squeeze and to cuddle. Include some toys or balls that make a sound when shaken – maybe because a bell is embedded in the toy.
- Have a set of simple containers and objects that can be grasped and put in and out, again and again. Try a plastic food container box and cotton reels, medium woolly balls, wooden or firm plastic spoons, and some lids.
- Sit with babies on your lap and let them touch you: your face, your hair, scrabbling at your collar or touching your jewellery. When their grasp gets stronger, gently unlock their fingers if they hurt.
- Babies like shiny pictures in books - to look but also to scrabble at with their fingers. Use cardboard books and let the baby decide when to turn the page. Make your own shiny book with A5 size plastic envelopes and put a bright magazine or calendar picture into each one.

The human gym

In the second half of this year, babies need to feel with their hands and their feet and then to experience full body movement. Hold babies with feet firm against your lap and allow them to bounce. Enjoy their energy and abilities with them.

- Lie on the floor and let babies crawl over you. Or sit and let them lean against your back. Play crawling-chasing on a soft floor – a game that involves you crawling after mobile babies (and toddlers too) and them chasing you on all fours.

Water play

- Most babies like the feel of warm water. You can offer similar experiences to bath time with babies fairly dry on the sidelines. Inevitably you will both get at least a bit wet, so have a warm dry towel at the ready.
- Sit with a baby on your lap and a shallow container of warm water on a low table. Or else sit on the floor with the baby, whatever will be safer and more comfortable in your setting.
- Let the baby watch and push about some floating bath toys. Push a toy under the water a little and then let it bounce back up.
- Let a sponge soak up the water and then squeeze it out from a small height. Show your appreciation of the

stream of water with 'Ooh, look.' Encourage the baby to put a hand into the flow.

■ Make little waves and mini- whirlpools with your hand so that boats or ducks bob and swirl. Encourage babies to imitate you when they are able.

■ Pour some water from a small plastic jug or toy watering can. Let the baby watch and put a hand or her fingers into the flow as it splashes into the bowl.

■ Hold an empty plastic bottle under the water and create bubbles as the water drives out the air. Empty the container from a suitable height and, if the baby looks interested, do it again.

■ Use appropriate baby bath mix to make some bubbles that the baby will try to touch and catch. Check with parents of babies that they are neither allergic nor sensitive to bubble mixes before you add these to water play.

■ Provide very small amounts of water on the baby's highchair tray or a table top to be hit, splashed and pushed about a little. This game may be part of your wiping up after meal times.

Learning through the sense of smell

Developmental focus

Smell is probably the most underrated sense and, like touch is far more than a physical sense. When a newly-born baby enters the world, their sense of smell plays an important role in the bonding process. Within a week, babies can distinguish their own mother's and another mother's milk on breast pads placed near their nose. Even within the early weeks, babies will turn their heads away from smells that they appear to find unpleasant

Pause for thought

Adults often overlook the experience of smells and different scents as an interesting event for children. However, the ideas here need to be approached as a resource, used over time. Of course babies or young children would feel overwhelmed if you ran through the ideas in quick succession.

Before doing any smell activities with babies (or older under-threes) do check with parents if the children have any allergies. Be prepared to have this conversation again, since some allergies and sensitivities take time to emerge. If there is any concern for a baby or child, then place the perfumes, petals, and so on, on small sticky-backed address labels, which can then be worn.

Look for the opportunity that slightly older children could help you make some of these 'smelly' resources – or other ideas in this book. Older twos and the over threes are often very interested to do something 'for the babies'.

Babies have limited clear vision beyond their focussing point and need to make sense of what they hear. So, new-born babies may rely on smell to give them a better understanding of the world, of what is familiar and unfamiliar. Through their sense of smell they can gather information about where they are and who is the person close by or holding them. A baby will be aware of different smells as you take them from one area to another, both in the nursery and outside.

Familiar smells can be emotionally significant for a baby and young child. For instance, never wash a baby or child's comfort 'blanket' or special cuddly toy without checking with parents. Unless an item has been washed regularly from the outset, you have to do your best through sponging off any spillages.

Let's notice pleasant smells

■ As well as special experiences involving smells, be alert to everyday smells, such as warm milk or food. Show the baby you are enjoying the aroma and say something like, 'mashed apple, my favourite!'

■ Experiment with different oils and essences in a safe burner. Watch the babies (and toddlers) to see how they experience the scent. Continue with those they seem to like and – obviously – discontinue the experience if any baby does not like this kind of scent.

■ You could hang oranges with cloves around the playroom. Another time, make mobiles for cots/ changing mats using pot pourri or herbs.

Bags of perfume

- Sprinkle fresh herbs and spices on to individual nappy liners, wrap them with different, brightly-coloured pieces of tulle and tie them with a length of ribbon.
- Dangle the bags one at a time in front of the baby. Encourage the baby to reach out and draw the scented bag towards his face. Let the baby play with the bag and experience the smell.
- Alternatively, put wooden scented fruits or flower petals inside the bags.

Smelly socks

- For this activity, you will need brightly-coloured baby socks, cotton balls, a length of elastic and pleasant spices such as cloves or cinnamon.
- Shake a pleasant-smelling spice on to the cotton balls and put them inside a sock. Tie the top of the sock and sew elastic on to the top, hanging it above the changing table or cot.
- Pull the sock and offer it to the baby or toddler. Once they have experienced the smell, let the sock bounce. Encourage the child to pull the sock towards his nose to smell it.
- To extend this activity put fruit, vegetables or pot pourri into the socks. Decorate by drawing faces on them or sewing some bells around the top.

Scented tissues

- You will need a box of 15 to 20 citrus-scented tissues. Give it to the older baby (or toddler) and let her pull out the tissues. (This item should not go into their mouth.)
- Take tissues that have been pulled out from the box and show the child how to roll them into balls, encouraging her to copy.
- Play silly games with the tissue balls. Put one on your head and let it fall off. Let her try the same.
- Put as many as you can in your hand and scrunch them, say 'Abracadabra' and open your hand so the balls can fall out.

Listening and enjoying sound

Developmental focus

Babies have a well-developed sense of hearing from birth, although of course they have to make sense of what they hear from voices and the sounds of everyday life. Babies will have heard many different sounds in the womb, including their mother's heartbeat and her stomach rumbling. It is important for parents to talk even with newborns, because the sound of the parents' voices helps in the bonding process. Babies need to be able to focus on sounds and to distinguish slowly the meaning of everyday routine sounds.

Most babies will be startled by loud sounds, so the gentle quiet approach is more appropriate. But also be alert to the temperament of individual babies. Some like vigorous bouncing games, along with a lively sound, whereas others like the energy and volume turned down a bit. A continuous sound encourages the baby to turn her eyes toward the noise, and shaking a rattle or repeating her name encourages a baby to listen and find the source of any sound – not always obvious to young babies. It is important never to persist with a sound or other game that seems to make the baby uneasy or jumpy.

Listen and look

- Play different kinds of music at various times of the day. Be alert for signs that individual babies recognise the rhythm of particular pieces. Be selective and avoid having continuous background music. It becomes unhelpful sound 'wallpaper'.
- Hang rustling kites, mobiles or wind chimes from the ceiling.
- Create basic sound makers from plastic bottles filled with pasta, bells, rice, beads and so on, making sure the lid is firmly fixed. It is a good idea to have at least one bottle that is visually interesting but does not make a sound – for instance, because it is filled with cotton wool.
- After a little while, if a baby does not pick up the 'quiet' bottle, then pick it up yourself, along with a 'noisy' one. Shake one bottle at a time, look puzzled at the 'quiet' one and comment something like, 'no sound at all'.

Noisy mobiles

- Collect a wooden or padded coat hanger, bells, string, foil, milk bottle tops, rattle, cellophane, sweet wrappers, beads, brightly coloured thin ribbons and one large wooden curtain ring.
- Attach the items tightly to the coat hanger with the ribbons. Ensure that one ribbon is much longer than the others and attach the curtain ring to the end of the longer ribbon.
- Hang the mobile above the baby's cot or resting area so she can reach the curtain ring and use this as a handle to shake the other items.
- Talk to the baby about what is going on and the lovely sounds being made.

Musical gloves

- Sew small bells on to a brightly coloured pair of gloves, one on each glove.
- Give the baby one glove at a time and urge her to shake her hand. Then give her both gloves.
- If she is enjoying this game, tie brightly coloured ribbons with small bells to the baby's wrists. Take them off as soon as the game is complete.

Instant percussion

- Make a collection of plastic containers, wooden boxes, saucepans, biscuit tins, wooden spoons and metal spoons, plastic egg cups and a sieve.
- Sit the baby on the floor and place a variety of containers within her reach. Offer her a spoon and allow her to beat the various containers.
- Join in, talking about the noises and sounds being created.
- Lift two of the egg cups and bang them gently together. Offer them to the baby and allow her to experiment.
- Use a spoon to run round and over the surface of the containers rather than beating. Offer a spoon to the baby and again allow her to play.
- Let older babies explore simple, real instruments such as drums, castanets and maracas.

Pause for thought: when to worry

Some babies will have disabilities related to the senses. It is not always easy to recognise visual or hearing loss in very young babies. However, parents and other key carers are usually the first to observe that something is amiss.

- Use your observation skills to be alert to babies who do not appear to react to sounds or do not gaze in the way that is usual.
- Babies usually respond to all the senses, although they will be less responsive if they are tired, hungry or unwell.
- Share your concerns, with care, with a parent and listen if they have worries. The parent may welcome your support in seeking an expert opinion, if you are both concerned.
- You also need to share any wariness about sensitivities or possible allergies that become clear through everyday care routines or games with babies.

Language and creative development

Babies make their mark

Developmental focus

Babies' interest in artistic and creative materials is stimulated by the interest for all their senses as well as their early attempts to manipulate materials themselves. It is important to allow very young children to learn how to use a wide range of materials at their own pace. They are discovering their world in terms of 'what is this?' and 'what can I do with that?'

Babies exercise their flair for creativity long before they are able to produce recognisable paintings or drawings. They enjoy opportunities to explore and experiment with colour, shape, texture and pattern. Babies learn about these qualities by hands-on experience for many months. They will hear words relevant to the experience from you, as a playful companion in their creative enterprises. Over time, your comments about 'a lovely swirl', 'do you want some more red paint?' or 'that feels soft' will make sense as a toddler's own language develops.

Artistic appreciation

■ Share books with babies that have interesting patterns, textures, colours and shapes. These features will usually be part of good illustrations.
■ Carry babies to look closely at pictures or posters on your wall. They often like to stare at 'real art'. Make a few comments such as 'I like that' or 'can you see the big flower' - and then point to it.
■ Interest babies with simple pictures, shapes and patterns. Laminate these and make them available – either to lie flat on the floor or hanging from ribbons tied firmly to either side of the picture.
■ Young babies especially like simple images with contrasting colours. Make a collection of paper plates which you have painted in geometric patterns with black against the white plate. Fix some images to a piece of doweling, so you can hold them up to show a baby.

■ Allow babies to explore different textures by making a mural they can touch. Include satin, silk, wool, cotton, corduroy, velvet, sandpaper (not too rough), tissue paper, textured wallpaper and so on.

Sensory art

■ Baby, and toddler, art is a full body experience. Keep the activity simple and remove all a baby's clothes except the nappy. Let them get their hands into paint or other artistic materials. Provide large sheets of paper or let them create impressive swirls of their own choice. Take a photo of the enjoyable experience to share with parents and keep for the babies to enjoy when they are older.
■ Put yoghurt, whipping cream, instant whip or baked beans on to a baby's high chair tray. (Do not use raw kidney or other beans that have to be cooked. These beans have a toxic ingredient that is only removed by boiling.) Let the baby feel the texture and experiment with the patterns they can make.
■ Make different coloured jellies. Place blobs of jelly on a piece of paper and let the baby mix them together.

Pause for thought

This section offers suggestions that include using food as a material that provides babies with sensory feedback and which can also be used for satisfactory swirls and designs. Some practitioners are uneasy about using foodstuffs in this way.

One reservation is that young children will then play with their food at mealtimes. Our experience is that children do not usually confuse artistic, hands-on play with mealtimes. If you do find that crossover is a problem, then stop using any materials that have confused any child. Babies and toddlers get their hands into their meals anyway. Slightly older children can follow a conversation along the lines of, 'this is uncooked pasta, so we can stick it easily' or 'the toddlers are having fun sitting in the flour. But we're not going to make cakes with it afterwards.'

The other objection is that many children in the world do not have enough to eat, so it is unethical to use food other than for eating. We agree with Penny Tassoni (in our personal communication) that, for logical consistency, this argument should then be extended to water. Globally, many families are desperate for clean, accessible water. However, the objection to food as a play resource is not extended to water play. Early years provision should avoid being wasteful, but families who need food and clean water will be best helped by donations to relevant charities.

- Mix a little washable paint and water with cereal, for example Weetabix. Place this mixture on the baby's high chair tray.
- Babies can safely put the food into their mouth but not if it has been mixed with other materials, like paint. So ensure that you offer one kind of 'artistic resource' at a time. You can then gently dissuade babies, if they should not eat this resource. The experience will then not confuse them.

Musical babies

Developmental focus

Babies experiment with making sounds that are pleasing to them. They make and enjoy patterns of sounds that have musical rhythm. Restless babies are often calmed by adult singing or from hearing gentle, quiet songs. Adults can build on this sensitivity to musical tone and rhythm by singing lullabies, nursery rhymes and chants. Babies

start to recognise familiar songs that are tuneful, brief and contain repeated lines. Babies and toddlers like a wide range of songs and music, not just those designed exclusively for very young children.

Babies will be startled by loud sounds, so a gentle, quiet approach is most appropriate. As their ability to manipulate objects develops, babies become interested in particular objects with which they can make sounds. They relish their ability to make something happen, in this case a noise of some kind.

Singing while we 'work'

- Of course nappy changing and dressing routines need to be safe and hygienic. But this time is also part of warm communication with a baby. You can sing a song or simple rhyme along with this playful exchange. Songs like 'round and round the garden' have movements that are part of the sung words. However, babies are very happy with a sing-song accompaniment that can be as basic as 'here we go, here we go.'
- While putting on clothes, play a little game. "Oh, where's Ben's hand?, Here it comes, here it comes, Oh!" or say a little rhyme, for example: 'blue socks, red socks. Cover up your toes. Green socks, white socks. Warm and cosy toes.'
- Part of your regular song can be that you put the baby's socks on your ears or trousers on your head. Simple visual jokes work a treat with babies.

Sing and dance together

- Hold the baby securely – on your lap or in your arms as you walk about or gently sway. Smile and look into their eyes.
- Sing a variety of songs, with different tempos and sung in an expressive way. The songs may be nursery rhymes, but they can be folk songs or anything that you know and enjoy singing.
- Change the baby's position between verses or songs. Make the singing interactive by touching parts of the baby's body as you sing.
- Hold the baby and dance to different types of music. Try out fast and slow music, loud and soft music, pieces with high and low sounds. See what individual babies like the most.
- Bounce the baby on your lap in time to the music. Change the baby's position as you listen, holding him over one shoulder, then the other.
- If babies are secure to stand up by holding onto a low table, see if they want to bounce to the music, while supporting themselves. You will notice that some older babies already have a sharp ear for the rhythm of a lively song.

Simple music makers

- Be creative in your resources for sound making – for instance build a collection of old sets of keys. They make a satisfying rattle when shaken or dropped into a little tin.
- Tie bells securely to a baby's gloves or booties to encourage them to make a sound by shaking hands or feet. Take the items of special clothing off the baby when the game is over.
- Playing with spoons offers variety for sound-making. Give the baby a wooden spoon and enable them to bang it on different surfaces. Different sounds emerge from thick paper, a table top, tin foil, cellophane and on a woolly jumper. Let the baby try the same sequence with a large metal spoon. Give the baby a metal pan to bang on using either of the spoons – but maybe not all on the same day!
- Make musical mats with about ten coloured face cloths. Firmly sew a variety of objects onto them, such as bells, buttons, scrunched-up silver foil, cotton wool and bubble wrap. Sew all the face cloths together or leave as individual mats.
- Sit the babies beside the mat or surround them with the smaller ones. Give them a large spoon and allow them to use the spoon or their hand to make a sound. Show them how to make sounds if necessary.
- Adapt this activity by placing a bed sheet or large sheet of thick paper on the floor or grass. On one area put sand or salt, on another cotton wool and on a third silver foil. Let the baby move about exploring sounds they can make.

Pause for thought

Many play experiences for babies do not lead to any kind of end product. Parents are interested in what their baby, or child, has done while they are in your care. You share some of those highlights through conversation. However, photos are immensely useful within your partnership with parents.

It is definitely good practice to take photos and to use a selection within your setting as well as share the images with parents. (Practitioners are sometimes given a contradictory message – usually when someone generalises from the position taken about a student's portfolio.) Nursery staff and childminders should always ask parents about taking photos when the family first joins any provision.

Stories for babies

Developmental focus

Telling a story or looking at books with babies is a time of emotional and physical closeness. A baby feels the warmth of attention from the adult through this shared activity. You support babies' emotional development, when you return to their favourite books or stories.

Good stories, story-songs and story-rhymes for babies unfold with a recognisable rhythm, that even under ones start to recognise with a big grin and perhaps waving of arms in pleasure. This experience helps babies to tune into sounds and sound patterns as they occur in everyday speech. This phonological awareness, enjoyed without pressure from the early months, lays secure foundations for spoken language. Oral communication is a crucial part of the knowledge that will help children - much later – when they are able to understand the written form of their language(s). So enjoyable stories and books with babies are a vital step on the road towards literacy.

Listen to the rhythm

- Even very young babies enjoy a story told through song, rhyme and gentle touch. They start to tune into the sound and rhythm of your voice long before they recognise the individual words.
- Try out different song- stories with babies, such as 'Pat-A-Cake', or 'See-Saw Marjorie Daw'.
- Be alert to individual favourites. A smile or happy sound will tell you that even a three or four month old baby now recognises and likes a particular song. Share this learning with parents and invite then in turn to share their knowledge of their baby.
- Extend your range of more conventional lullabies and rhymes for babies. However, many babies like 'grown up' story songs, such as old music hall favourites like 'Daisy, Daisy'.

Stories with movement

- Create some simple hand movements or gentle touch to fit a baby's favourite song or rhyme and keep to the same pattern whenever you tell this story. The baby will start to anticipate the gestures, soft tickles or being bounced on your lap or along your stretched out legs.
- By the time babies are six to eight months, try a definite pause before the final line of a story song, or the hand movement accompanying a rhyme. See if the baby looks expectant and then enjoy the final words or gesture with her.

■ Babies and young children need you to look as if you are enjoying yourself just as much as them – so, if necessary, you need to get over feeling self-conscious. Babies are not music or theatre critics! Just be expressive in how you sing or say the rhyme.

Books for babies

■ You need to be close to babies when you tell a story in any format. They should be on your lap or you can be sitting together on a sofa or cosy corner on the floor. Babies cannot share you and a book with more than one, at most two, other babies.

■ You will face babies when you tell a story through song or rhyme. When reading a book together however, ensure that you are both looking at it from the same angle.

■ Tell the story at the pace of a baby or very young child. Sometimes she will want more time to stare at the picture, touch an illustration and feel any special parts of a book designed for touching as well as looking.

■ Select a few suitable books to share together but be ready to follow a baby's own choice as soon as she shows a preference

■ Leave the stronger board books easily available for babies, so that they can choose and look whenever they want. Books with paper pages can be kept in a basket or higher shelf and brought out when you can easily show how to handle them gently. If possible, have the less robust books so that babies can see them and finger-point to make their request.

Physical development

Getting on the move

Developmental focus

Babies gradually develop the ability to control their limbs and whole body in a deliberate way. It takes time and active practice for them to build up muscle strength until they can hold up their heavy head. Further effort is needed to be able to sit up securely – an ability that frees the baby's hands for exploration. Further effort brings the success of mobility, by various methods of rolling, crawling, bottom shuffling and eventually walking. Older babies are then truly on the move and delighted to be able to head off for interesting objects and sights within their familiar learning environment.

Pause for thought

Young babies need all the necessary support for their bodies that they cannot yet provide themselves. In the early weeks, this means safe support for their head. As their physical control moves down the body then they need a different kind of support. Babies need a safe seat for parts of their day, or for times when they are travelling in a car.

However, babies who can hold their head up need to spend some time (awake) on their stomachs on a comfortable floor. With interesting resources, like an adult, close by at their level, babies have reasons to practise lifting their head and shoulders. Also being on their front is the ideal position from which to move into the all fours mode and try to crawl.

Safety advice is to put babies to sleep on their back and not their stomach. But this direction does not apply when they are awake, and their muscle strength has developed so that they can lift their head and face from the surface.

Baby exercises!

- Mobile babies want and need to practise their skills and they become more confident through a fair amount of repetition. Provide them with safe space and admire what they manage.

- Create a well-padded area with lots of floor space where the babies can move around. Be prepared to play on the floor with babies, enjoying the play materials or letting them crawl all over you.
- Create a 'mountain' with cushions, bean bags and pillows in a pile on the floor. Allow the baby to explore the mountain of scattered cushions. Pick up a cushion or roll over them and the baby may copy you. Hide behind the cushions and play some 'peek-a-boo' games.
- Encourage use of baby gyms so they can stretch up, swing arms and kick legs. Sometimes it is you who dangles something over baby's feet to encourage kicking.
- Let babies move freely on a variety of textures - a pile carpet, linoleum, or fresh, clean grass. Get down and join babies as they creep, crawl or shuffle.

Baby reach

- Dangle a variety of objects above the baby's head to encourage stretching.
- Play with toys just beyond the baby's grasp. This will encourage the baby to stretch and explore the items when they retrieve them.
- Treasure Baskets (see page 9) develop larger scale movements as babies reach for items in the basket, waving and shaking them. This enjoyable resource also gives babies practice in sitting unaided, or with safe back support, when they are ready.
- Use your collection of plastic bottles with different contents (see page 10). Place them on a large carpeted area where the baby can stretch, touch and explore them freely.

Bouncing rhymes

- Sit the baby on your lap facing you. Hold the baby under his arms and move forward until you are sitting on the edge of the chair.
- Lift your heels so the baby gets a good bounce while you recite some bouncing rhymes, such as, 'Horsy, Horsy' or 'Yankee Doodle'.
- Sit on the chair with your knees crossed. Rest the baby over your foot and grasp her hands firmly. Lift your leg up and down. Keep your foot close to the floor and the baby eventually will push her feet off the floor in response.

Flying games

- Try these games when babies can hold their head up on their own.
- Lie on the floor and gently lift the baby up and down. The same game can be played with you in a sitting position. Some babies may prefer that version, or you may be less confident about the muscle strength in your own arms, especially to 'fly' a heavy baby.
- Holding your hands under the baby's armpits or around the chest, move the baby backwards and forwards from side to side.
- Move the baby in all directions. Slowly and gently dip the baby's head and then feet towards you.
- If the baby likes this game add some bounces, lifts and wiggles. Talk or sing to the baby.

Pause for thought

When you are attentive to babies, you will notice what they think and feel about an activity that you have introduced to them today. You will need to follow their lead over how long they want to play a game, and within the bounds of safety, what they are keen to do with the resources you have provided.

But their reaction today also lets you know whether this game should be offered on a regular basis. An enjoyable game should not only be for one time only. Sensible observation-led planning is created by simple alertness. Babies will let you know that they want, for instance, to play funny faces in the mirror again, because they point or bring you the hand mirror. A basket full of ribbons can become part of the baby's daily range of choices. When you notice that a resource is met with enthusiasm by one or more babies, then the wise decision is to put these materials in a container at their grasping and pulling height. The only reason to place the basket or box higher would be that play with this resource definitely needs an adult right by the side of a baby.

Through relaxed observation – your listening and looking – you can ensure a flow between activities that you initiate, and maybe lead in the first instance, and those that are initiated in a freely chosen way by babies or toddlers.

Seeing, reaching and grasping

Developmental focus

As well as the larger physical movements, babies are developing their finer control, in combination with vision and touch. Fine physical activities and skills are those that involve small muscle movements in the hands, feet and mouth, often in co-ordination with the eyes. A baby gradually develops the ability to concentrate and control these movements, but first has to realise that her body parts belong to her.

Any activity that stimulates the hands will help babies realise they are in control of them. They start to play with their fingers, while focusing their eyes on them, from around three months. During the second half of the first year, babies experiment with different ways of exploring materials through physical manipulation and they tend to use their favourite method on anything. Babies explore through holding, squeezing, throwing and dropping, rubbing and scrunching, turning over and around or poking. They do not know enough about the world to keep themselves safe, nor to distinguish play materials from valuable adult possessions, so that is your job. By their first birthday most babies will reach out to grasp objects and put them in their mouths. They start to manipulate objects with increasing control using the pincer grasp - the co-ordination of the index finger and thumb.

Grab, push and pull

- Hang mobiles so that the baby can reach towards them and stroke the baby's palms to encourage clasping. When a baby has clasped an object in one hand, pass her another object to encourage use of both hands.
- Activity centres and mats may encourage babies to push, pull, dial, prod, screw and hit. You could also let them play with old telephones, either with dials or touch pads.
- Place some set jelly in a tough plastic bag or rubber glove and tie it securely. Let the baby experiment with it.
- A treasure basket (see page 9) encourages babies to develop their fine motor skills as they explore and play with the different objects.

Pause for thought

Babies will use their current favourite method of physical exploration on any object of interest. Your role is to enable them to explore and learn, while keeping them safe. Your attentive observation will also provide a sensible 'what next?' as you join in a baby's spontaneous play. The EYFS guidance stresses that supportive practitioners are responsive to child-initiated play.

In the early months the nerve endings in a baby's tongue, lips and mouth are more sensitive than those in their fingers. If you try to stop a baby mouthing, then you deny them information about their world. Just ensure that any freely available plaything is clean and not so small that they could swallow it. When necessary, gently encourage a baby to touch an interesting object with fingers only.

Watch how individual babies choose to explore their world? In what ways is their chosen method changing over time? Does this baby concentrate on turning an item around or over? Does another baby, even of a similar age, put energy into stroking or shaking. Does another baby rub, drop or try to scrunch up the items within reach?

Your friendly observation lets you make a sensible offer of play resources to individual babies. For instance, if a baby is struggling to scrunch up a rigid plaything, then you need to push across something that will give way to little fingers. If a keen baby is able to tear the pages of a book, then gently replace the book with some paper than can be torn and ripped.

So many ways to explore

- Hang a colourful silk scarf loosely around your neck and dangle the end of it in front of the baby. Encourage the baby to grab and pull your scarf off.
- Throw scarves or tissues into the air, for the baby to reach out and grab.
- Collect enough lengths of ribbon to fill a small basket and offer this resource to babies. Watch what they do with the ribbons. Encourage some possible ways of exploring by pulling out one or two ribbons yourself. Make an interested 'ooh' sound or look surprised at the length as a long ribbon just keeps on coming. Be ready to show that ribbons can be pulled, felt, draped over your head or over a cuddly toy.
- Make a 'washing line' as you tie a length of string at a very low level and drape different types of material, in strips, over the string. You might do this indoors or outside, in fair weather. Encourage the babies to reach towards the strips of material and pull them off. Stay close all the time and take the line down as soon as the babies show you that the game is complete, as far as they are concerned.
- Play 'fill it up!' by placing the baby in a comfortable position and giving her a container. Let her look over the array you have created by scattering hair rollers, dolly clothes pegs (the old-fashioned kind that do not have the metal hinge), crayons or fir cones around her. As you play, encourage the baby to pick up objects and place them inside the container. Drop a few from a small height to make a satisfying sound.

Serious hands-on fun

- Place a large bowl of cooked (and now cool) pasta on the floor and sit one or two children either side of it. Let them explore the pasta and maybe lift it into other, smaller bowls and then back. Watch how they enjoy the slippery texture.
- Another time, try the same experience with soft cooked jelly or try either material in a larger-scale version and let babies and toddlers have the pasta or jelly in a container that is large enough for them to sit in the jelly.
- Put sand into a large enough container so that more than one baby can sit in it. A good option is to have one of the wide, flat tuff-spots (or builders' tray). You can spread a generous layer of sand and babies can sit in it, wriggle their toes, try to grasp and scrabble. Gently ensure that they do not eat it.
- Try generous amounts of flour as an alternative. Babies or toddlers need cleaning up afterwards, but being sponged down is part of the fun. Be especially careful about flour going into a baby's mouth if there is any chance of an allergy, or simply use a gluten-free flour that you know is safe for anyone.

See what I'm doing!

- Babies become interested in watching the movements of other people. You can play a face workout when you sit the baby opposite you. Show them a smile, a frown, make a sad face, look surprised, and see if the baby joins in.
- Watch any baby, or toddler, carefully – obviously you stop if they experience this activity, or any facial expression, as no fun at all.
- You can add noises to go with the expressions. Or try the variation that you cover your face with your hand or a cloth and each time your face is revealed, your expression is different. This activity is not only for babies; toddlers and young children often find the changes hilarious.

■ Follow any funny faces that the baby makes. Babies and young children are usually enchanted if you sometimes follow their lead.

■ Explore similar actions by using a hand-held or fixed wall mirror if the baby enjoys this variation.

Pause for thought

Babies, and young toddlers, cannot manage to play with the larger water or sand trolleys. A collection of smaller containers will be useful for offering any natural substances, including water. Apart from the tuff-spot builders' tray, you can use a baby bath placed on the floor, washing up bowls, seed trays (without holes), the large lower containers that come with equally large plant pots or litter trays (designed for use with cats). Babies and young toddlers can access these containers easily. It is an advantage for very young children that there will not be many other babies or toddlers around the resource. If an activity is popular, then you need to set up more than one smaller container.

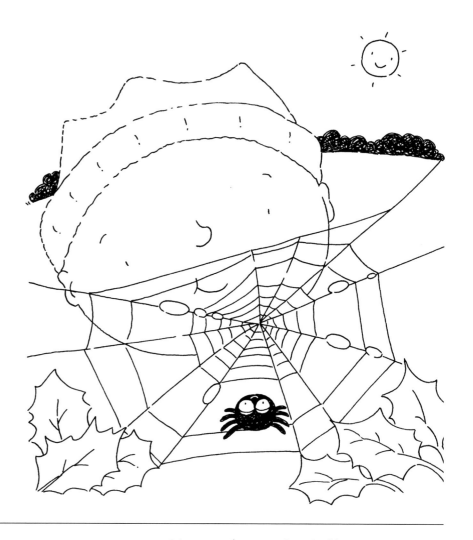

Using the environment

Getting outside

Developmental focus

Babies are ready to be interested in almost anything and there are rich sources of learning outside as well as indoors. By two to three months babies are well able to focus beyond their close visual field and to be intrigued by sights at a slight distance. Over the following months their head and body control steadily enables them to turn to what catches their attention and to reach out and touch objects.

In the second half of their first year, babies' increased mobility means that you have to watch them carefully in the garden, as anywhere else. However, since you will be there enjoying the outdoors with the babies, this should not a problem. Babies will benefit from getting out in the air and you need to wrap them as warmly as they need for the day's weather. In summertime the issue is sometimes more that of being cool enough and keeping young babies out of direct sunlight. A simple canopy is often the answer, along with any natural shade in the garden.

Sight and sound
- Find a sheltered place in your garden that still means babies can watch what is going on and lay out a thick rug or other ground covering for you all.
- Try to see the garden from the babies' viewpoint. Lie on your stomach alongside the babies who can lift their heads to look around. Sit with them or hold babies on your lap as they sit or stretch up on their legs supported, to look forward or over your shoulder at what is happening behind.
- Watch and listen with the babies, enjoying what intrigues them. Ask them, 'what can you see then?' and 'is it the birds?'
- Enjoy the sight and sound of swooping and chattering sparrows, coloured blossom, petals falling to the ground or the trees swaying.
- Add some visual and sound points of interest to your garden such as wind chimes and other sound-making mobiles, flags or streamers that will catch in the breeze.

Watching the world go by

- If you have a front yard or step, sit out with the babies and wave to passers by or watch the neighbourhood cats.
- If the entrance to your nursery or family home is on a busy road, then try watching from a window.
- Comment simply on what you both see and express your enjoyment as well. Sometimes follow the baby's gaze and other times call her attention to something interesting with, 'ooh, look.'

What's that?

- Walk a baby about the garden, stopping to show them flowers or a pet if you have one. Drop some petals or leaves for the baby to watch float to the ground.
- Select some items of interest that they can touch, like stroking soft leaves or smelling a flower. Make sure plants are not pulled into the baby's mouth and wipe their hands afterwards.
- Towards the end of the first year, babies who cannot yet walk alone, like to be hand walked around the garden. Go at their chosen pace, looking, listening, smelling, touching and commenting.

Comfortable outdoor surfaces

- On a warm enough day, take some of the babies' books and play materials out onto the rug and enjoy their usual play in the fresh air.
- Enjoy physical play on the rug. Try some gentle body wrestling with the babies, or let them crawl over you as you lie flat out and under the tunnel you make when on your hands and knees.
- Thick blankets or thin duvets can create a soft base for babies who lie or sit. Slightly older children are often pleased to help you 'make a cosy corner' for the babies in the garden.

Babies and children usually love playing with water and they need easy and safe access to it. This resource is a useful example of the importance of sensible, and not over-anxious, risk assessment. Water poses a risk because babies and young children can, and have, drowned in even very shallow water. But the point is that these tragedies happened because an unsupervised baby or child was able to move to and fall into water and a responsible adult was not right there to prevent the accident.

The potential danger of water as a play resource is reduced to zero when young children are watched carefully when they are close to water, even if it is only a few centimetres in depth. Your responsibility is always to be very close at hand – children are never left in or by a paddling pool or pond, even for what seems like the shortest of times.

■ Containers like the tuff spot or a baby bath can provide a secure and dry sitting place, as well as being a good surface to put play resources or hands-on natural materials for enjoyment outdoors.

Outdoor water play

■ Take advantage of warm weather and let older babies paddle their feet or sit in a safe paddling pool in the garden. Stay very close and watch them all the time; do not turn your back even for a few seconds.
■ Babies enjoy the sense of having few, if any clothes on and splashing the water vigorously. Give them some plastic cups or other containers to play with. Pour some water over their arms and legs.

Views on the big wide world

Developmental focus

Within the first couple of months the visual field of babies remains relatively close to them. But soon their interest is caught by what is happening further away in their immediate environment. Trips out for babies offer close and affectionate contact between adult and baby. There is also the healthy impact of getting outside and the stimulation to learning offered through new sights and sounds. If you work in an area with poor air quality, you may want to select your routes with care but do find

some. Younger babies may simply enjoy the movement but, once they can comfortably sit up, older babies are ready to take in the local sights and sounds.

Adults need to get out as well as babies and toddlers, or else it can seem like a very long day. Very young children are ready to be delighted by what seem like very ordinary outings to adults. You need to re-capture that sense of when everything was new: buses are interesting, so are local cats and gurgling water after a rainfall. Babies will not be critical about where you go for your local trips, so long as you are on the move and you talk with them.

Getting out together

■ Tired, bored or fractious babies are often soothed by the rhythm of being walked in a baby carrier or pushed in a suitable buggy or pram.
■ Babies in a carrier enjoy the contact of being physically close and the reassuring sound of a familiar voice.
■ Talk with babies and pay attention to how they respond. The trip is also a time for personal communication.
■ Make sure that you regularly make warm eye contact with babies. Give a smile and a friendly word. Tell them where you are going and what you are doing. Of course, they will not understand your words but your affectionate tone will involve them.

Outings are a shared activity so it does matter that babies feel that their important adults are fully involved in this experience. Some people feel strongly that backward facing buggies would be a significant improvement and help babies and toddlers to communicate with the adults pushing the buggy.

Our feeling is that buggy design is not the key issue here; the main point is that adults (parents or early years practitioners) are committed to communicating with the little person sitting in the buggy. Disaffected and disrespectful adults are unlikely to change bad habits by facing a baby or toddler. It is an even worse message of rejection, if a baby can see the face of an adult and that adult is more interested in talking on their mobile or with another adult pushing in parallel!

There is a logical point to backward facing prams or carrycot transporters for the months that a young baby can only lie down flat. A communicative adult can easily catch their eye and chat. However, once babies have the muscle control to sit upright, they are alert to the sights of a local trip. They will not get the best views of their neighbourhood if they can only see what they have passed by and not what is coming up in front.

What can you see?

- Get down to the eye level of babies in a buggy or pram, not only to communicate with them, but to see the environment as they do.
- What can they actually see and is it interesting? Will it help to adjust how babies are lying or sitting? Do you regularly need to line up the buggy or pram for an interesting sight?
- Turn the buggy to face an intriguing shop window or a wonderful display of blossom. Move the buggy close to something of interest that the babies can swipe at or touch.
- Stop regularly during a local trip and look with the baby from their angle. Check what has caught their attention and share their visual interest. You give an early boost to babies' sense of self worth when you show pleasure in what has excited them.

- Invite babies to home in on one or two new sights with 'oh, look! Do you see the bird on the fence?' or to listen with, 'What's that noise? It's a fire engine. Look here it comes!'
- By nine or ten months, babies may start to recognise some features of a local circuit. Share their pleasure as they point out a familiar landmark or kick their legs with anticipation as they recognise the last metres before the bakers or getting back to nursery or home.

From One to Two years of age

Development within the second year

Within the months between the first and second birthday a toddler moves from looking and behaving like a large baby to appearing more like a very young child. Toddlers' individual temperament is becoming ever clearer and their own wishes are expressed firmly by gesture, other body language and their emerging words. Toddlers' close relationships with family and other carers are important to them. They show affection to familiar, loved people and distress at separation or new and confusing situations. Toddlers want to feel part of their daily life and they can learn much through happy involvement in their daily routines. Of course they can learn a great deal through play. However, adults who offer, 'do you want to help me?', discover how much toddlers enjoy being trusted to have a role in domestic events.

Toddlers' ability to understand and express themselves is supported by adults and older siblings who take their early communications seriously. Alert adults can easily see the impact of toddlers' previous experience on what they do. These very young children show evidence of remembering, some planning ahead and thinking about what to do and how to make something work. Their play, creative exploration and emerging language is more than simple copying of what they have seen someone else do or heard them say.

Toddlers are absorbed in using all their senses and want to practise and extend their physical capabilities. They are inquisitive and open to any appropriate challenges to explore and learn. They still have a limited understanding of the how the world works. So caring adults need to keep them safe, without undue restrictions and to be realistic in their expectations. Adults need great reserves of patience as they help toddlers to learn about where and how they can play and what is off limits to them

Toddlers cannot yet take care of themselves so adults need to ensure the young children's health and well being through adequate rest, nutrition, hygiene and emotional care in a calm and secure environment. Adults who value their nurturing role will help toddlers' all round development.

Developing relationships

Early communication

Developmental focus

Communication moves towards words because familiar adults and older siblings respond with enthusiasm to those sounds that are close to real words. Many toddlers' first words appear somewhere between twelve to eighteen months, but it is very variable. Toddlers are growing in their understanding as well as their ability to express themselves. They need adults who communicate clearly with the toddlers, give them time and patience and help them to link familiar words and phrases with understandable events of the day.

Words are learned because they are useful to the toddler and carry meaning in their environment: the names of people and objects and words like 'more' or 'no' that help the toddler to control what happens. Toddlers use a small number of words but they convey a lot of meaning because of the supporting gestures and expressions. Toddlers' mistakes in how they use words are usually logical; perhaps all furry animals are a 'cat'. Listen and watch the toddlers and you will usually be able to track, with interest, how they have made their sensible errors. Towards the end of this year, many toddlers start to combine two words.

Let's have a chat

- Toddlers enjoy short conversations with adults who are genuinely interested. Give your full attention, listen to what the toddler says and all the gestures that add to her meaning.
- Expand what she says with a few words of your own. Keep your questions simple, friendly and linked with what interests the toddler and what is visually obvious to her.
- Help toddlers to communicate with each other. Let them try to make contact before speaking up on their behalf. Enjoy their give-me games and other play, with limited words, by watching from the sidelines.
- Local trips help toddlers recall a route and look ahead. They will enjoy the anticipation of 'Here comes the post box. Are you ready with the letters to post?' and 'Yes, there's our special big tree. Do you think we'll see the squirrel today?' Toddlers will show that, in a meaningful

context, they understand words from you that they do not yet use in their own speech.

Make the links

- Support children as they make connections in their world and begin to voice these in words or show through communicative gestures and other behaviour.
- Be pleased that a toddler shows how she remembers with, 'well done. That's where we keep the crayons. Which ones would you like?'
- In the second half of this year, toddlers begin to link the picture of something with the real object. Be ready to help this process as you look at books and posters, 'Yes, there's a banana. That's one of your favourites' or 'It's the big red bus. We saw one of those this morning.'
- Involve toddlers in the daily routine so that they can learn about sequences (what do we do next?) and predict what is needed, by helping you lay the table for lunch or tidy up ready for tea. Make plenty of materials available for them to enact this experience in their pretend play.

- While you are dressing or changing a toddler's clothes, describe what you are doing. Name each piece of clothing as you put it on. Try to follow the same familiar order. Say little rhymes, such as, 'where are your fingers?'
- Let toddlers help to dress or undress themselves. Watch them to see what they can now manage and acknowledge with a simple, 'Well done!' or 'Look at you – you've put your hat on.'

Spot and say games

- Sharpen up toddlers' 'looking' skills and their understanding of useful words with finding games. Make a collection of familiar toys and objects and play 'Where's the....?' so that toddlers point out or bring the cup, ball or doll.
- You can play the same game with parts of the body or clothing. Be enthusiastic with, 'yes, well done, that's your nose!' or, 'yes, that's your shoe…. and that's my shoe.'
- Within the second half of the year, toddlers will enjoy looking, spotting and naming with simple pictures or wall posters. Encourage them with comments like, 'let's find the..'. 'where's the…, I wonder' or 'what's that in the corner there?'
- Make a set of pictures of familiar objects and laminate the images. Spread out a few pictures and try a game of 'where's the …?' See if a toddler can look carefully over a larger array of images and find the familiar object that you request.

The social life of toddlers

Developmental focus

Toddlers will have developed an understanding of who is familiar in their daily life and who is not so well known or a completely new face. They are able to make close relationships with adults within and outside the family and with other children. Toddlers need some predictability and continuity in their lives for healthy social and personal development. Too many changes or the arrival of unknown carers can block their willingness to make contact; life is too uncertain.

Very young children think of themselves as individuals and you need to treat them as such. Clear respect for their individuality will enable toddlers to develop their social self as well. It is a myth that very young children only engage in parallel play. If you watch them, you will see that toddlers make contact with each other, play together and sometimes develop their own simple games with a friend or sibling.

Making friends

- Toddlers can feel secure enough to make sustained social contact with other young children. Watch them and notice the friendships that are developing.
- Help them to learn the names of other children and key people in their lives. Play 'where's…? spotting games with the names of children and adults.

Pause for thought

The EYFS stresses the importance of the emotional environment, as well as an interesting and accessible indoor and outdoor learning environment. This backdrop of warm adult behaviour and a commitment to nurture creates the possibility of pro-social behaviour – an element in some of the early learning goals for PSED and five-year-olds.

Toddlers are ready to be caring towards others and helpful within the daily routines, although not all the time, of course. Young children grow in sensitivity to others when they have experienced a genuine concern for their interests from adults. Toddlers need a nurturing environment in which they do not have to fight for adult attention. Very young children will then start to develop what is called pro-social behaviour. This pattern is the beginnings of an awareness of the feelings and needs of others and the wish to support them.

- Young children are sometimes brought together because the adults (childminders, nannies or parents) enjoy each other's company. Do not insist that the children must be friends too. Sometimes they may not get along at all.
- If you are in a nursery it is important to have quiet areas for young children. These can be your cosy corners, where it is easy for toddlers and children to settle with a book or toy, or with another child. Toddlers will often spend some time together, lolling on the cushions and enjoying the sense of a 'den' that is created with drapes and maybe soft lighting.

Social mealtimes

- Eating together is ideal, as young children are influenced by what they see others eating. Make meal or snack times a social occasion. Sit with toddlers and keep them proper company, even if you are not always eating at the same time.
- All young children appreciate attractively presented food and like to help adults to arrange the table or a plate of items.
- You can create a warm and playful atmosphere without inappropriately turning meals into playtime as such.
- Toddlers and young children often like to keep each other company and chat when they are in the bathroom. You need to ensure that individuals who like more privacy are respected. But sitting on the pot or toilet, or washing hands is often a conversational time for children.

Playing together

- Give toddlers space and time to develop their own games in which both have a role to play.
- Watch and be encouraging about toddlers' give and then take back games or their pleased imitation of each others' physical skills like waving gestures or jumping up and down.
- Set up some activities in which more than one child can play together. It might be very simple dressing up with hats, making faces or funny movements in a large mirror. It needs more than one person for a good hide and seek game or building up a brick tower and then knocking it down.
- Help children by having enough play materials that turn taking is not too great an imposition. Supplement your bought play resources with baskets of everyday objects and recycled materials.

Finding a social role

- Toddlers want to be part of what happens and are only too keen to have a helpful role in the domestic routine of home or nursery.
- Find the many safe possible ways to show toddlers that you welcome and trust their skills. Let them tidy up with you, fetch you something simple from across the room, hand out the banana slices or pat the baby's hand.
- Always say 'thank you' or 'well done' for the toddlers' help. They will soon follow your good example and express similar warm feelings to each other.
- Look for opportunities to give toddlers choices and the chance to express an opinion in words and gestures. It might be to choose a story or a book or where to stick a picture on a board or wall.
- When toddlers tell you someone is crying, respond to their concern and thank them for bringing it to your attention. Acknowledge their attempts to comfort their peers, for instance, offering a stroke on the hand or fetching another toddler's comfort blanket. You can say, 'Katie was happy to have her teddy. Thank you for being kind to her.'

Using the senses

Seeing, exploring and understanding

Developmental focus

Toddlers are able to focus on objects at a distance as well as close to and this ability supports them as they recognise familiar faces easily and point to objects and events of interest. With this developed visual awareness, toddlers enjoy looking at simple picture books and touching familiar items on the pages, as well as exploring almost everything in their familiar environment.

Looking around and scanning with interest are important aspects of the development of concentration in a very young child. Toddlers will often sit or stay still for some time when they – the children – are very interested in something. You need to provide plenty of hands-on experience and let toddlers see, as well as feel, the qualities that they will eventually (but not yet) describe with words for different colours, shapes, textures and other abstract concepts.

The helpful adult role now is to use your spoken language so that toddlers hear the words to describe such ideas, at the same time as they can feel 'rough', see 'green' or hear 'noisy'. Very young children are able to and enjoy sorting items out by 'same' and 'different' long before they can link real objects to abstractions like colour. Their looking and touching skills are a vital first step.

Wall hangings

- Buy or make different kinds of wall hangings and see-through pockets. Household stores, DIY and warehouses often have cloth storage systems that work well for children's purposes.
- Fix any wall pockets at toddler eye height and put items of interest in each pocket – a book, one toy or a picture.
- Encourage toddlers and young children to look closely with 'what can I see there?' or 'I wonder what's in there.'
- Help toddlers to get out the item if they need assistance.

Well spotted!

- Young children are able to start playing 'hide and seek' - let them watch you hiding the first few times until they understand the game. If they hide, then obviously do not find them too easily.
- Larger boxes are also ideal for regular peek-a-boo games, when you have cut interesting shapes all over the box. Let children go inside to peek out and let others peek in.
- Have on hand a rich variety of simple picture books to help develop this interest. With only one, or at most two toddlers, play spotting games for familiar items within a picture or poster.
- Toddlers begin to understand the names of things before they can vocalise them. So use their visual skills as well as their understanding and ask questions in a playful way such as 'where's the..?' and 'what have I done with the...?' Try a few deliberate mistakes in familiar routines and ask, 'What's wrong here?'
- Get some large paper plates and cut out the centre. Show toddlers how it is possible to look through the hole – at someone else or to see only part of a large picture. If they enjoy these windows on the world, then cut some different shapes out of more plates.

Coloured frames

- You need cardboard frames of various sizes (15 cm x 15 cm, 20cm x 20cm and so on), coloured gels or cellophane, and everyday objects such as fruit and toys.
- Tape or glue the gels or cellophane to the cardboard frames. Then encourage the children to hold the frame up to the front of their faces. Or hold it for them.
- Place one item at a time in front of the frame, and let them look at the unusual image. Ask the toddler, 'what's happened?' and use the colour word as information, 'it's gone all green!'.
- Swap frames so they can look through different colours and ask questions or make comments to stimulate toddlers' interest and their response.
- Extend this activity by making coloured spectacles using cardboard frames and cellophane. Encourage them to play with the glasses on. Alternatively, use sunglasses, making sure they don't have prescription lenses and supervising the children closely.

Mirror games

- Enjoy play with mirrors – whether it is a hand-held safe mirror or low wall mirror that can reflect several toddlers.
- Play a game with toddlers of making faces in the mirror and see how swiftly they make this game their own.
- Make portable reflective boards with sticky back reflective paper. Or cover a table top that can stay as a 'mirror' for some time.
- Let toddlers sit on top of the reflective board and enjoy what they see and the images as they move around toys or natural materials like leaves.
- Use the reflective table top to enjoy different materials. One day it might be hand-painting and swirls onto the surface. Another day it could be shaving foam or a cornflour mix.

Touch and feel

Developmental focus

Toddlers still put objects into their mouth but this is now more for exploring taste and texture and often for comfort. They have now learned what many familiar objects feel like. So they may stretch out for their favourite cuddly toy, grasp and pull it to them, confident from the feel, not needing to look. Toddlers' skills of touch combine with more visual confidence so that they manipulate objects to see what will happen and to repeat an action, often many times with obvious delight. With improved hand-eye co-ordination, toddlers can experiment in deliberately bringing objects together, putting small objects into different containers and feeling for relative size and shape.

Toddlers still themselves use and welcome touch as a means of communication. They want to be close to familiar adults, especially if they feel uncertain, tired or unwell. They also use touch to make contact with other children and can be helped to be more gentle, if necessary. Toddlers are also in the process of learning what they should not touch, but it is a slow process. Be patient and show them what is safe to look at but not to touch. They may even spontaneously learn helpful phrases like 'not for me' so that they are more able to guide themselves.

Lots and lots of 'stuff'

- Collect a rich array of recycled materials such as cardboard boxes, tubes, large curtain rings, corks, dolly pegs, lidded boxes or tins. Store these in separate baskets or boxes - instead of mixing items in a single treasure basket.
- Store the containers on an accessible shelf or area and enable toddlers to access the baskets when they wish.
- Maybe have some special boxes, decorated in good quality wrapping paper and ideally with lids. Bring out two or three of these surprise boxes from time to time. Part of the enjoyment is a slow lifting of the lid and saying, 'what's in our surprise box today?' The contents can be different each time but are not conventional toys.

Feel and find

- Put four of five familiar objects into a cloth bag and let toddlers feel inside and then bring out the toy, cup, brick or other object.
- Encourage them to feel and think about what they can touch with, 'I wonder what it is?' or 'is it the ball, then?' Don't press toddlers to guess, although they may start to try.
- When the object emerges, say, 'you touched the cup' or 'you got the spoon'.
- Join in their interest at which item or toy they have discovered and have a go yourself, perhaps make a mistake or seem uncertain.

Feely books and mats

- Make a cloth book with different pages made of varied squares of material. Encourage toddlers to feel, stroke and rub the different textures.
- Collect different textures of paper and similar: wallpaper, popper wrap, shiny wrapping paper and stiff brown paper. Let toddlers scrunch up the sheets and then bat it around like a ball.
- Collect materials that look as well as feel different: velvet, brocade, thick cotton, wool and flannel. Cut them into squares, with sides of approximately 15-20 cms. Use pinking sheers to stop the fabric fraying. The squares can be stored in a basket or firm-sided cloth box.
- Alternatively you can fix the materials firmly over cut out card and sew or glue the material on securely. Toddlers can still stroke the materials and can choose to lay them out like a patchwork mat.
- Explore the different materials with toddlers and young children. Show how it is possible to stroke each one, hold it against your face or run just one finger over the surface.

What does it feel like?

- Let toddlers experience water in its different forms: when it is still, a regular drip or a steady pour. Feel the difference between wet and dry: a flannel or sponge, material, tissues.

- Use your language to comment on 'how does it feel?' and to use the words for warm, cool, tickly – whatever is the sensation.
- Blow some bubbles, chase, touch them and feel them pop.
- What does sticky feel like: a blob of jam or sticky tape. Explore the feel of soft and squishy with play dough.
- Explore the feel and ways of manipulating mixtures: knead bread or pizza dough, shape and roll biscuit dough. Then cook and eat it too.
- Introduce the words for different textures and feels, but do not expect toddlers to learn and remember them yet. Their enjoyable hands-on experience will build the basis so that the words eventually have real meaning.

Smelling and learning

Developmental focus

Smell seems to be the sense that many adults take most for granted. Yet toddlers are aware of familiar smells: pleasant or unpleasant. The smell of fabric conditioner on a blanket may remind an individual toddler of home. Their wish to hold onto something that belongs to Mummy or Daddy seems to be as much about smell as familiar sight. Toddlers will not have the words to explain these links but the sensation will be part of their daily experience. Their facial expression, gestures and a few words will tell you they recognise a smell and whether this recognition brings pleasure.

Smells may bring unhappiness or uncertainty, for instance if they are associated with ill health or medical procedures for those toddlers who have spent time in hospital. Partnership with families should ensure the open communication that lets you know that particular smells, or noises, are likely to cause distress. See the general comment on page 12 about possible allergies.

Enjoy the smells

- Toddlers can find the act of deliberately smelling something quite difficult. When asked to smell something, young children sometimes blow out through their nose. It is useful to teach the child to blow out through their mouth so that they will breathe in automatically through their nose.
- Make a treasure basket with citrus fruit (oranges, lemons, limes). Pierce them with a fork to produce a stronger smell. You could also include wooden fruit and pine cones.
- Offer the children empty containers in which the smells still linger, for instance: cosmetics, shampoo and bubble bath.

- Let children play with a variety of herbs and flowers with smells that will remain on their hands for a while.

Everyday aromas

- Encourage children to use their sense of smell on everyday experiences and materials, for instance, food and drink, common toiletries in your setting or toothpaste.
- Make fruit juice, and encourage the children to smell and taste the fruit.
- Take regular opportunities to prepare food with young children and let them smell the jam or butter, tomatoes or fresh bread.
- Alert toddlers to smells that communicate events in the day, such as 'I can smell our lunch' or 'here we go, can you smell the swimming pool?'

Pretty smelling pictures

- Gather together a selection of fresh herbs or flower petals. Put them into small tubs and secure the top. Let the children smell each tub.
- Put a little of each herb (or petal) into the child's hand.
- Let them sprinkle the herbs (or petals) on to a piece of paper. Alternatively, let them sprinkle the herbs (or petals) on to pre-glued paper and let the children smell and touch their pictures.

Washing hands

- Place three bottles of scented soap with different odours on a table. Place a blob of each - one at a time - on to your own hand. Invite the toddler to smell each scent.
- Place a small amount on to the toddler's hands, gently rub into her palms and encourage her to smell the soap. Talk about the smell and feel of the soap while rubbing and rinsing the bubbles from her hands.
- When dry, ask her to smell her hands again. Can she still smell the scent?
- Let the toddler choose her favourite soap with which to wash her hands. Alternatively, wash each hand with a different scent.
- Put some of the soap into a small container of water, allow the toddler to swish the water until bubbles appear, let him place a piece of paper or material over the bubbles, then smell the print.

Natural outdoor smells

- Buy some pots or boxes of herbs. Let the toddlers hold or lean over the pots, while you comment on the smells.

- Encourage the toddlers to bend and smell each of the herbs. Let them touch and feel the herbs, rubbing the leaves to make the scent stronger and let the smell linger on their hands.
- Allow each child to select and pick one or two herbs and place them in a pot or wrap them in damp tissue to take home.
- Create a more permanent source of smells by planting small herbs plants or flowers with definite scents. Involve the toddlers to help water and care for the special garden and to smell the plants as they grow.
- Use the children's selection of herbs during a baking activity.
- Go on a woodland walk and let the children experience the smells of leaves, bark, logs or wood shavings. Accept that some country smells are not pleasant and the toddlers may show their disfavour.
- Go on a seashore walk to experience smells such as the scents of shells and seaweed or of fish. If you are a long way from the sea, then ask anyone making a seaside visit to bring some items back with them.

Hearing and listening

Developmental focus

Toddlers need to develop their ability to listen. This skill along with looking, forms crucial building blocks for their ability to concentrate. Unlike babies, whose attention is often naturally distracted from one object to another, toddlers can focus very deliberately on items and events of interest. They often want to repeat, or have you repeat, something interesting again and again. It is important to follow their request, since toddlers learn with repetition and practice.

Toddlers are able to distinguish between voices and sounds and can recognise simple tunes that have been sung many times by a parent or carer. When you talk with and listen to toddlers, your attention will support their language development and they will add to their vocabulary. Speech is a social skill within toddlers' development, so it needs to be encouraged within genuine conversation with adults and friendly older children.

Sound spotting

- Have a good store of rhymes that become familiar to toddlers so that they can recognise and respond to the opening sounds or words. Add to your repertoire by asking parents to share their rhymes and songs.
- Whenever possible, draw the children's attention to noises and sounds that have meaning in daily life.

Pause for thought

Good early years practice is to offer resources and suggestions to toddlers and children. The activities in this section are especially attuned to exploration through the senses. However, when you try any ideas, it is important to use this time as an opportunity to watch and listen to the toddlers. Their experience of discovery supports many aspects of young learning, not only developing a particular sense.

Even if you know these toddlers very well, there is no way you can predict in advance what toddlers, twos or other young children will do with an experience initiated by adults. Nor can you predict, with any useful certainty, what the children will learn this time. You can only gain a sense of likely learning by observing what is actually happening. The EYFS emphasised the importance of observations and in the context that children's learning flows across every area of development.

Today the toddlers may show you that they are utterly fascinated by the perfumes. But they may be keen today to use some novel resources to their own play purposes. They may deliberately practise movements that build specific physical skills. On the other hand, they may spend more time communicating with you or with a friend through give-and-take play. You may realise, perhaps in the children's enthusiastic help when tidying up resources into the different boxes, baskets and bags that they have a clear idea of categories. They are sure that the tubes all go together, the shells go in the special basket and the chains go in the pretty carrier bag.

You might call attention to the sounds of the dustcart because it is the day that the dustbins are emptied or to a baby calling out in the next room.
- Sometimes just sit in peaceful silence in the home, garden or playroom for short periods of time. What can you hear? You will notice that there is rarely complete silence.

Shake, rattle and ring

- For this activity, you will need a sheet of plywood, and items such as a bicycle bell, motor horn, door bell, buzzer, door knocker and old style telephone dial (if you can still find one). Attach all the items to the front of the board, making sure they are secure.
- Invite the toddlers to have a look and try the items out.
- Once the children have had time to explore the noises, you can join in.
- Have a basket with duplicate, separate items that the children can play with too.

Grab a noise

- Collect a variety of fabrics, such as fur material, kite fabric, foil, bubble wrap, a length of cotton wool, sand paper and cellophane.
- Place the fabric in a large box. Then sit the toddlers down beside the box and invite them to look at what is inside.
- Take one piece of fabric out at a time. Let the children take the fabric and squash it and pull it. Alternate the fabric, bringing out one that will make a noise, then one that will be silent.
- Encourage children to make a noise with each of the fabrics. Describe the feel and the noise it makes as children experiment.
- Once all the fabrics are out, let the children play with them however they wish.

Playing about with sounds

- Sit two or three toddlers down beside you in a quiet place and make different sounds for their entertainment.
- Make a variety of noises, such as 'oohh', 'aahh' and 'eehh', and encourage the children to copy. Make the noises quietly at first, then louder, then quiet again.
- Say hello in a funny voice and encourage children to copy. Follow their lead and copy any funny sounds that the toddlers want to make.
- Explore any song or rhyme that could be enjoyed by varying the volume from very quiet to noisy.

Pause for thought

During this year, it will become clear that some toddlers are not fully confident in using their senses. Although it can be hard to assess visual or hearing loss in young children, it should now be more possible to pin down potential worries.

- Talk with parents, listening to any concerns that they express and sharing your own observations.
- Toddlers with partial or total visual loss will benefit from adjusted play activities as well as your awareness of how not being able to see will affect how they can understand their world
- In the usual course of events, toddlers should be using some words that are recognisable to familiar carers and should be responding to meaningful sounds. If this development is not happening, then hearing loss has to be one explanation to be considered.
- Be aware of toddlers who have many colds, especially if this includes ear infections. The bouts of ill health can mean that their hearing is intermittent, which confuses their learning. Frequent ear infections can damage hearing.
- Continue to be aware, with toddlers' parents, of any possible allergy or sensitivity that emerges through exploration of touch and smell.

Language and creative development

Artistic toddlers

Developmental focus

Toddlers are interested in creative activities because such play satisfies their wish to use their physical skills and to experience through all their senses. They are also intrigued by their ability to make something happen, either to make interesting marks, to squeeze play dough or to create a simple collage that is then displayed and admired. Toddlers relish and learn from the creative process and they need to be given scope to use materials as they wish, within the confines of safety, of course.

Toddlers are ready for mark-making with short, fat, non-toxic crayons that are easy for their hands to grasp and that provide immediate results. Thick paintbrushes or foam wedges are easier for them to hold and give scope for satisfying sweeps of colour and texture. In using play dough or suitable clay, toddlers may sometimes make something but often learn a great deal through manipulating, pushing and poking the materials.

Art made easy

■ Have generous resources so that toddlers do not have to wait for a tool or a single pot of paint.
■ Tape large sheets of paper to the floor and let the children make marks on it with thick crayons.
■ Large areas of paper, like wallpaper rolls, enable bigger scale toddler murals.
■ Have a wide array of larger brushes and paint rollers - you can buy little rollers in DIY shops. Over time let toddlers experiment with different mark making tools: twigs and short lengths of dowelling, shower scrunchies, wedges of foam or feathers.
■ Gather large cardboard boxes and encourage toddlers to decorate them with a range of mark making tools.
■ As an alternative to bottled paint, make a thick paste from cornflour, water and food colouring. Give them a small tray of this paste to draw in with a short piece of doweling.

Pause for thought

Very young children can be truly creative responding to the opportunities that you make available. Creative activities are a good example of the importance of good ideas from adults, offered to young children as opportunities to explore and not as 'have to do' sequences. The EYFS emphasises that there needs to be a balance between activities started by adults and those that arise from the genuine choice of young children.

Some very enjoyable creative enterprises for toddlers and twos will be adult-initiated – started by the grown-ups – and maybe also adult-led the first time around. Young children will discover some uses of materials themselves but many of their skills will be supported by an experience that was set up by an adult.

Children cannot ask to do an outdoor rubbing 'again' - or know which resources to get out - until they have experienced this activity at least once. They may come up with ways of painting with a shower scrunchy that the adults have not predicted. But for this creative leap, toddlers and twos need that first time when adults put some shower scrunchies on the table alongside paper and paint. The adult will also have been ready to model what might be done with a scrunchy and showed interest at the mark that she or he did make.

■ Make marks on fabric using a range of materials – ask parents to donate old tablecloths or sheets. Use the design to drape over a display table.

Taking art outdoors

■ Fill shallow trays with a mixture of powder paint and sand. Take the trays outdoors and encourage the children to draw in the sand with their fingers. They can shake the trays to erase their drawings and to start a new one.

- Set up a blackboard at the children's level and provide a range of chalks for them to use. Take boards and easels outdoors as a regular event.
- Paint an area of the wall at the children's height with blackboard paint – it can always be repainted.
- Provide water and encourage children to water-paint outside – on a surface like paving or a wall. Water painting can be extra interesting on a warm or hot day, because the art dries out quickly.

Paint dippers

- Cut squares of material 15cm x 15cm, place cotton wool and a piece of sponge in the middle, gather corners and tie up into a small sack shape with string.
- Pour some paint into a paper plate for them and show toddlers how to dip in their paint applicators and then print onto paper.
- Crumpled paper or cotton wool balls can be used as an alternative. To add texture empty satsuma bags may be used rather than pieces of cloth.

So many kinds of finger-painting

- Clear a table-top at the children's height or sit them on the floor. Let them explore the texture of the paint with their fingers. Encourage them to use their fingers, fingernails, fingertips, knuckles, thumbs and palms to produce different effects.
- Try variations around this creative theme. You could add aromas - for example, cinnamon, lemon essence or washing-up liquid. Add textures: sand, tea-leaves, woodcarvings or desiccated coconut. Add colour with powder paint, poster paint or glitter.
- Try finger painting with instant pudding mixes, hand lotion or shaving foam.
- Paint onto different types of paper: embossed wallpaper, corrugated card and newsprint.
- Finger-paint directly on to the table top then, if toddlers want, take a print of it using a large sheet of paper.

Textured collage

- Gather a range of types of pasta: shells, bows or spirals. Select the bigger sizes, as these are easier for toddlers to manipulate. Let the children put glue on to paper and create their own design with the unboiled pasta.
- Pasta can be coloured by adding a few drops of food colouring and shaking to mix.
- Rice, lentils, dried peas and many other dried foods can also be used for collages. Avoid any beans that the packet instructions tell you have to be boiled for a certain time when they are cooked. Uncooked, raw beans of this kind have a toxin that is poisonous if the beans are eaten.
- The sticky side of sticky-backed plastic can be used as a base for younger children and avoids the need for glue. This option also works if children want to make a smaller collage.

Musical toddlers

Developmental focus

Toddlers will start to use words within this age range and they enjoy sound making, rhyme and rhythm. Some toddlers will enjoy trying to sing parts of songs, others may mouth or whisper the words. Many toddlers will indicate that they want a favourite sound or piece of music even if they do not have the exact words. Toddlers may also become so focused on the actions for songs that they will not yet sing along, being more interested in the hand or body movements. Each child will develop at a different rate but all can have an interest in and enjoyment in musical sound making and listening.

Sing along

- Let parents and carers know the songs and rhymes you are using in the nursery by photocopying them on to attractively decorated fliers so that the children can enjoy them at home too.
- Make sure that families know you welcome ideas in return. If you live in a diverse community, families may be a rich source of music and song from a wide range of cultural backgrounds. Tapes and CDs can still help you select musical resources to reflect the broader society for all children.
- Provide a wide range of opportunities for singing, listening and moving to music, as well as using instruments to create sound. Consider making musical push-and-pull toys as well as using bought musical instruments or sound toys.
- Use songs as a way to learn about parts of their body, for instance, 'Head, shoulders, knees and toes', 'If you're happy and you know it' or 'The hokey cokey'.
- You can often make songs personal by using the names of individual children.

Shake it all about

- Give out large paper bags and encourage the children to decorate them using large marker pens. With the children's assistance, put a small amount of rice, lentils, beans or peas in the bags.
- Tie the bags with wool, making sure you leave plenty of room for the items inside to move around. Then let the children shake the bags. Comment on the sounds that emerge.
- Your store of plastic bottles will be a fine accompaniment to singing as well as general rhythmic sound making. Ensure children can easily choose one or two bottles with different kinds of materials securely inside.

Dangly music

- Attach a wooden or metal curtain pole at a height giving toddlers easy access. Or place the pole securely between two A-frames.
- Attach a variety of sound-making objects to the pole. Make them secure and without loose strands.
- Choose items that can be shaken, knocked, bashed or banged and that will make a selection of sounds. Possibilities include a string of bells or beads, four wooden clothes pegs on a string, conkers, small metal spoons, a whisk, an empty plastic bottle and a plastic bottle with lentils or rice inside.

Song box

- When you introduce children to new songs, it is helpful if they have something visual to recognise and link with the song. Use a large bright box to store a visual aid for each song. You can have pictures but young toddlers will probably be more engaged if the visual aids are 3-D, for example, soft toys, dolls, puppets or models.
- Introduce the object at the same time as the song. The children will begin to realise that the cuddly brown dog means they are invited to sing 'How much is that doggy in the window?'
- Create a box with three or four items that support songs the children already know. You might have a padded star for 'Twinkle, twinkle', a rag doll for 'Miss Polly', a plastic duck for 'Five little ducks' and a spider puppet for 'Incy wincy spider.'

Tell me a story

Developmental focus

Stories can have become a valued part of the day for toddlers, who enjoy choosing and listening to familiar and favourite books. Toddlers relish books shared and read out loud by an adult, but they also like simple story telling without a book. Stories can also be told through songs, poems and rhymes.

Repetition within a story and having favourite stories many times help even very young children to anticipate, recall and join in as they wish. Old favourites may be learned almost by heart and simple tales told to photo or picture books may even be repeated meaningfully by toddlers as they look through the book on their own. The rhythm of a good story or rhyme continues to support toddlers in their language development and crucial listening skills.

We love books

- Make enjoyment of books a personal time, with close attention to one or two toddlers. Be ready to sit and read a story or tell a story-song like 'Miss Polly' when toddlers ask.
- Be ready to do it again and again. Children learn stories by more repetitions than you would probably choose. Be just as expressive each time you tell or sing the story.
- Pause at appropriate times in the telling of a tale, especially where there is a sense of 'what's coming next?' Pause and look expectant – toddlers and young children soon join in repeating a phrase or question that is part of the story.
- Help toddlers to learn care of books by showing them how to turn pages and by not leaving out easily torn books. Gently remove books that are treated as balls or sucking objects.
- Make books easily available to the children, on a low shelf or table or in a broad open container or basket. Books with pulls or flaps may be better in a special box that comes out on request and when an adult can sit with the child.

Recognising and asking for stories

- Watch out for how individual children ask for a known story. They may bring you the book they want, use one or two words that hint at the title or maybe try a gesture from a story song's hand movements.
- Keep a record of the stories, through any medium, that a very young child requests and see how it changes over time. Share this information with parents and welcome their account of what happens at home.
- Take some photos of toddlers enjoying a book, listening to your story or making their first attempts at hand movement to a story song or rhyme. The photos will be enjoyable now for you and the child's parents, but also keep them safe for the child to enjoy when a little older, as part of the personal story of 'what I did when I was little.
- Have a special bag in which favourite books can travel between a toddler's family home and nursery or childminder's home.

Telling a tale to pictures

- In books with just photos or drawings create your own story line and tell the same sequence each time. Keep it simple, with some examples of 'Ooh look at...' or 'Where's...?' Try an anticipatory 'and then....' or 'I wonder what will happen..' as you turn a page.

- Look for opportunities to build familiar sounds into your story line: cats who meow, cows who moo or babies who cry.
- Listen in when children choose to look at this book on their own; you may well hear some of the story you created.
- Be ready to share a special story line with colleagues and parents, because young children are likely to require the 'proper' story told to the pictures.

Stories through rhyme and song

- Add steadily to the children's repertoire of story songs and rhymes and learn new ones whenever you can from parents.
- Mobile toddlers may enjoy more active movements such as in 'Incey Wincy Spider', 'Ring-a-ring-a-roses' or 'I'm a little teapot'.
- Be ready to repeat a new, liked story rhyme several times so that the children feel they have got to know it well.
- Let children join in as they want - some will simply enjoy listening, watching and anticipating what will happen next.

Physical development

Energetic and on the move

Developmental focus

Toddlers have now developed considerable physical control compared with their baby months. Some may be walking confidently before, or soon after their first birthday, while others may need to be encouraged to begin. The timing of the first steps is very variable and it is important to notice and encourage toddlers through all the physical successes that happen before walking. Pulling to standing, cruising along furniture and tottering between the safe holding positions are all exciting events.

Toddlers need and want plenty of varied play experiences during which they can strengthen their arms, legs and body muscles. Their physical development is promoted when they have safe space and equipment to allow them to crawl, climb, walk, throw things and balance. Toddlers enjoy pushing and pulling wheeled toys and propelling themselves along on pedal toys such as bikes and tractors. They learn and practise the balance to pick up toys and carry them around and they are keen to start negotiating stairs and simple climbing frames.

Physical fun

- Offer safe space and plenty of practice; toddlers need to repeat actions and gain confidence over the weeks and months.

Pause for thought

Toddlers need friendly watching to keep them safe. They also appreciate plenty of encouragement from adults who value toddlers' physical achievements. The EYFS, and other early years guidance around the UK, is clear that physical development is equally important as other areas of learning.

Bursts of energy are normal for this age group and toddlers who are kept restricted or made to be 'quiet' will probably respond by persistent activity. Their growing skills open up the world for them, enabling them to explore without your assistance and to bring items and events excitedly to your attention. Use of physical skills, in play or within ordinary daily routines, can give toddlers immense pleasure and satisfaction. Watch them and you will see how important these skills are in the toddlers' personal world.

- Some toddlers are by temperament more wary or daunted by a tumble; they especially need caring adults to support them, offer practical help like holding a hand.
- Supply cardboard boxes large enough for toddlers to climb into and out again. They will enjoy this activity and it will help to promote co-ordination and balance.
- Provide wheeled toys that children can sit on to develop steering skills, balance and co-ordination.
- Organise outings to parks where children can use suitable play equipment or simply have fun running, jumping and shouting in the open air.

Ball games

- Provide balls of all sizes and of various materials to enable stimulate toddlers to move around and practise chasing, grabbing and holding.
- Roll a ball towards the toddler from across the room. Encourage the child to bend over, pick it up, and bring it back to you. Give a big hug and applause to motivate them further.
- Put a large soft ball in the middle of the play area. Kick the ball gently to show toddlers. Then encourage them to have a go. You may want to hold the ball yourself if toddlers are still unsteady on their feet.
- Encourage toddlers to move the ball in other ways: pushing, rolling or shoving along.

- Cut a large hole in a cardboard box and place it in the middle of the floor along with balls or bean bags. Encourage the children to drop or throw them into the hole. Cheer when they 'score.

On the move

- Toddlers often enjoy transporting items around their indoor and outdoor space. Provide different kinds of bags as well as trolleys and barrows.
- They may like transporting the collection of filled plastic bottles. Make a collection of padded Jiffy bags that you have filled with newspaper and sealed tight. These can be transported, delivered or thrown about.
- Provide pull-along toys to encourage children to walk for a longer period.
- Play running or crawling chasing games with toddlers. Make sure you move slowly enough that they can get away sometimes and can catch you.
- Blow bubbles and encourage the children to chase around – indoors or outside - and catch them.

Balloons

- Tie balloons to string and hang them up in the middle of the room, at a height so that children can reach them easily.
- Show children how to hit the balloons and make them swing.
- Make up games such as getting children to stand at the side of the room, run to the balloons and bat them with their hands.
- Balloon dancing can be encouraged by giving each child two balloons on short ribbons. They can twirl them, bang them together, or bounce them on the floor or grass.

Poking, piling and filing

Developmental focus

With increased fine physical control, toddlers can start to pick up small objects and manipulate them in a deliberate way. For example, they start to build small towers from blocks, manage very simple jigsaws and enjoy putting smaller objects into larger ones and tipping them out again, often many times. Toddlers like to use their physical skills to join in their own care and this early self reliance can give them much pleasure. They may be able to pull off their socks or a hat, perhaps pull up loose trousers. They are more able to feed themselves, manage drinks through a straw or suitable cup and control dribbling or drooling.

Fine physical skills are reflected in their play as they develop the ability to grasp crayons using their whole hand to make marks on paper. They may be able to handle a large paint brush when given the opportunity. Toddlers' interest in books gives them the opportunity to turn pages, sometimes several at a time, and to recognise and point to items on the page. Toddlers practise detailed physical skills within daily routines as well as play activities. They need interesting and varied play materials and lively adults who will play with them. These resources are enough for toddlers to apply and practise their growing abilities. They do not need organised physical programmes, unless a child has physical disabilities or a chronic health condition that affects movement.

Fine finger work

- Provide a wide variety of materials that allow toddlers to exercise their interest and skills in picking up and putting down, sorting, making piles, posting into containers and carrying around.
- Provide the children with empty, large cardboard boxes, which they can decorate inside and out with crayons.
- When reading books with toddlers, encourage them to point to and identify specific recognisable items on the page.
- Place large basters in a tray or basin of water and encourage the children to squeeze the water in and out of the basters.
- Set up a basin or tray of water and cut out small fish shapes from a range of interesting materials. Get the children to 'fish' out the pieces of materials using only their forefingers and thumbs. You can vary the experience by changing the temperature of the water, or adding bubble bath or non-staining food colouring.
- Put glitter shapes into the shallow bowl of water and let the children try to catch and pick out the shapes. Have a go yourself and make sure that you miss some.

Wonder boxes

- Collect a range of colourful boxes and put interesting objects inside them. You might add a variety of shells, coloured glass pebbles, a collection of plastic animals or a miniature tea set.
- Take your time in lifting the lid, with 'I wonder what we have here'. Then allow the children to take the lids off the boxes and handle the objects.
- These boxes would most likely come out for 'special occasions'. If you look after older children, involve them in ideas for what could go in the wonder boxes for the young ones.

Making a delivery

- Ask parents and carers to bring in old junk mail and make a post-box by painting an empty box red and cutting a slot in it.
- Let the children enjoy posting the mail through the slot and then allow them to empty the post-box and 'deliver' the mail elsewhere in the nursery.
- Wrap up toys with paper or cloth material and encourage the children to unwrap them to see what is inside.
- A similar activity can work if you collect special present carrier bags, or even plain brown paper deli bags. Toddlers and twos can hold these smaller bags easily - put items in and get items out again. Pull out one of your boxes or baskets with tubes or dolly pegs and see if toddlers would like to deliver those across the room or garden to you, via their little carrier bags.

Fingers-on play

- Gather a range of large uncooked pasta shapes (like cannelloni) that can easily be threaded on to lengths of string or ribbon. Toddlers can paint or dip the pasta shapes before threading – of go straight to making their pasta chain or necklace.
- Help develop the toddlers' fine motor skills by placing a range of malleable materials in a basin or sand tray. Choose materials that they can hold, squeeze, pull apart, poke, bash and roll.
- Watch and listen so you can be sure what has most engaged the interest of these individual toddlers. Consider making their favourite resources part of the

regular provision. Then also provide new ideas by some changes to the malleable materials and tools.
- Playdough is always popular with toddlers as well as older children. Add food colouring to brighten it up, essences to give it a fragrance or glitter, rice or sand to give it a texture. Gloop is another popular option.
- Cook up a mix of rice and add a flavouring like strawberry. Let toddlers have a generous pile each and let them poke it, squeeze it and if they wish move the rice around with a simple tool.

In and out – on and off

- Collect some spare large bottles from a water cooler – or ask the supplier for a few bottles for the children. These 'giant' bottles are ideal for posting corks, large beads and chains. They can also be hit with a wooden spoon or spatula. So long as they are fairly empty, they can also be rolled or lifted.
- Bring together a generous collection of dolly clothes pegs and large catering size tins (having ensured there are no sharp edges on the tin) or cardboard boxes that are not too thick. Model for children how it is possible to put a dolly peg onto the side of the tin or box. Offer the toddler a peg, encouraging him to try.
- Collect medium size wooden curtain rings and a wooden mug tree. Hang a couple of rings on the tree and let toddlers experiment.
- Offer a collection of clean hair scrunchies and a wooden or metal holder for a kitchen paper towel. Again put a couple of scrunchies on the holder and let toddlers explore.
- Fix a simple hook rack to the wall or onto a box. Put a collection of plastic bracelets alongside and hang one off a hook.
- Have a permanent hook rack and make a set of laminated photos of children's families with a ribbon holder. Hang the photos on the rack, with the full understanding that toddlers can take the photos off the rack.

Pause for thought

The ideas in this section are sure to interest some toddlers. You will notice that these very young children are individuals – the focus of the EYFS of The Unique Child. The Scottish Birth to Three materials are also strong on showing respect for a child's interests.

You cannot be sure in advance about what exactly will catch a toddler's attention and certainly not what they will, in the end, learn from an enjoyable play experience. The point is to make interesting materials available, be engaged yourself and share the lead with the toddler or young child about what happens next.

Using the environment

Getting outside

Developmental focus

Mobile toddlers want to explore the outdoors in their own way. They are fascinated by outdoor events and objects that may seem very ordinary to you. Watch the toddlers and you will see how ready they are to be intrigued and enchanted. Toddlers are soon able to learn words to name what they see and will use their emerging language to tell you about what interested them. They are learning about the world around them, what happens and how they can be involved sometimes.

Toddlers have no understanding of potential danger or hygiene issues, but it is possible to start their learning about care and cleanliness without restricting their explorations too much. They will respond to kindly suggestions to 'look but don't touch' for some objects. If any children have allergies or a tendency to sneeze at pollen or seeds, then clearly you adjust any experience accordingly.

Pause for thought

Older babies and children need sun protection – by a good hat and suitable lotion, which you will need to put on for them. But everyone needs enough sunlight, as a primary source of vitamin D. Children, or adults, who are thoroughly covered up and/or do not get outdoors regularly, easily experience the health risks of vitamin D deficiency.

Look and touch

■ Move around the garden or yard with toddlers at their pace. They cannot learn if they are rushed. Show an interest in what has caught their attention. Tune into what they want to watch or touch and they will learn far more than if it is always you who decides what is interesting.

■ You may think stones are boring but toddlers are often fascinated. Gently stop them putting anything into their mouth and, if need be, arrange a pile of smooth stones and shells that you washed earlier.

■ Encourage children gently to touch and smell flowers or leaves. Plant some aromatic herbs like lavender, rosemary or lemon balm to smell.

■ In the autumn, watch the falling leaves or seeds like sycamore 'helicopters' and blow on the white dandelion seed heads.

■ If your garden does not have any trees, then bring in a big bag of clean leaves and make a pile for the children. They can kick the leaves, hurl handfuls into the air and throw themselves into the soft pile.

Mini beast safari

■ Find out where the mini beasts live in your garden and soon the toddlers will revisit their 'homes'. You can show young children to take care of little creatures - to watch rather than poke or scoop up.

■ Lift a few large stones for the toddlers and watch what scurries out from underneath. Turn over the earth with the child's help and watch for the worms.

■ Create some inviting 'homes' by laying down a section of old carpet with the help of the toddlers and twos. Then go back on a regular basis to see what is happening underneath.

■ Keep an eye out for spiders' webs so you can watch them at work. Enjoy the magical sight of sunlight sparkling through dew on the web.

■ A feeder in the tree can encourage birds to visit your garden and stay long enough for children to see them clearly and recognise regular visitors.

On the move

- Create the space in your garden for toddlers to get moving with push along trikes and other wheeled vehicles.
- Provide small wheelbarrows for transporting any outdoor toys as well as some of the pile of leaves. The wheelbarrow can be the ideal equipment for toddlers who help to tidy up the garden at the end of outdoor playtime.
- Have a store of large cardboard boxes that can be anything the children want them to be, as well as offering the joy of climbing in, sitting down, getting up and out, over and over again.

Games in the garden

- Big balls, and ones that bounce easily, allow children to practise their skills of throwing, rolling and handing on.
- Play peep-bo around garden obstacles and simple hide and seek games in which you will have to pretend not to see the toddlers with 'where's Jamie now?' and 'where has Ayesha gone? I can't see her anywhere!'
- Running games start with a '1,2,3 go!' Chasing games can end in a big hug and swing up in the air for the child.
- Sometimes toddlers will chase you. Run slowly so that they can catch you.
- Experiment with fast and slow walking, turns to each side, big and little strides and walking backwards.
- Walk toddlers one at a time around the garden with their feet resting on your feet and your arms holding them secure as you do your funny walk together.

Catch and find

- Put various pieces and colours of silk or a similar material in a decorated box or bag. Demonstrate 'juggling' or throwing the material high into the air and watching the silk float slowly to the ground. Extend your arms to catch it.
- Use tissues, soft scarves, balloons or bubbles as objects to watch as they float and then try to catch them.
- Use bubble makers and help toddlers if they cannot make the bubbles themselves.
- Throw items or roll suitable items, so the toddlers have to watch and track the items in order to retrieve or catch them (toddlers are still learning to catch so make it very easy).

Water power

- Toddlers love pouring from one container into another. Their often repetitive play is a good way for them to practise this skill outdoors, when spillages do not matter.
- Provide containers with some holes, plastic sieves or small cutlery drainers so that toddlers can watch the water trickle out the bottom of these items. Have containers for water out in the garden, but also let children sprinkle water over the flowers in this way.

The toddler as traveller

Developmental focus

Toddlers are developing their physical mobility and, within the boundaries for safety in trips, they can walk some of the distance in a local outing or get out of the buggy at an interesting point. Toddlers are curious and ready to learn some names of what they see and hear. They will also point out items of interest to you. Toddlers have much to learn about the world and objects or events that are very ordinary to you can be novel and intriguing to them.

Toddlers often just enjoy getting out. So long as you keep them happy company, they do not require expensive trips. You need a break too and there are many possibilities, even in apparently unpromising areas so long as you think creatively. Young children are learning so much that is new; their task is often to make sense of it and explore how one experience links with another. Helpful adults look for ways to help toddlers to make those interesting connections.

Build up the ideas

- Check out all your local possibilities for free or nearly free outings and share ideas between colleagues and with parents. Perhaps keep a file of what is available locally for free and jot down opening times if relevant.
- All these ideas depend, of course, on careful adult supervision that keeps children safe without unnecessarily restricting their enjoyment.
- Think child-focussed timing for your outings - perhaps a half hour trip gets you all no further than round the block. However, the toddlers have been fascinated to watch two cats playing in a front yard, followed by the exciting sight of a mechanical digger working on the road. To them this is a really successful trip.
- You may have regular outings to the local park (even a small area will have something of interest for young children), the library, local shops or a market.

- Libraries offer a welcoming environment for browsing and also may have special events like story telling sessions or music.

Flexible plans

- By all means have a plan, but be responsive to the children's interests today, let them influence the schedule. Pause to look at what interests the children and build in regular local stops for sights that they enjoy and anticipate.
- Have a store of little paper carrier or deli bags, so that children can easily bring back any treasures, like leaves ,or their store of leaflets from the bank.
- Tell toddlers about your plans for this trip, for instance, 'we have these letters to post' or 'let's buy some bread rolls for tea'.
- Nurseries benefit from having a petty cash fund to provide for small purchases which give real life purpose for local trips for children.

Look and learn

- Look for safe vantage points to watch transport. Can you observe trains from an embankment? Young children enjoy this activity and waving to the passengers. On the street, look out for the less usual vehicles like fire engines, police cars and really big trucks.
- At different seasons there may be plants, flowering shrubs or young birds to visit by looking at local gardens, the park or recreation ground.
- Do not let rain stop you: umbrellas will keep off light rain. Ask parents to equip toddlers with small umbrellas, wellingtons and a suitable coat. Build up your own store by asking parents for any items they no longer want in their family.
- After rain, a local trip may be to tread in the puddles or make tracks with the buggy wheels. Or you may be lucky enough to have a rainbow. Wrap up warm in cold weather with snow and go out to make tracks.

Recognise and recall

- Toddlers, like babies, enjoy familiar experiences as well as brand new ones. Share their pleasure with your expression and words as they point out their favourite little fountain or the wall where the snails congregate.
- Support toddlers' memory and powers of recognition in a local circuit. Help them to see when you have approached a familiar landmark from a different direction: 'look, it's the garden with all the gnomes. We've come from the other side.'
- Take a series of photos of the route for a regular trip, or of seasonal events. Laminate the photos or otherwise

protect them for regular use. Use them as a photo set, or make into a book. Share with the toddlers 'here's the way we go to market' or 'this is our story of how the sunflowers grew so very big.'

Buying, carrying and collecting

- Show that you trust toddlers and let them hold something sometimes, perhaps the drinks and snacks for your trip to the common.
- Within the boundaries of hygiene, encourage toddlers to collect items of interest like stones, snail shells and leaves. Back at nursery or home, wash anything that needs to be cleaned and display the collection. Or use it in creative activities, as the children wish.
- At the post office or bank, they may like to select a few leaflets and forms. Toddlers like this paperwork just because it seems important to adults.
- Trips do not all have to have a shopping element, but small purchases can interest children. Involve them in the anticipation, selecting and payment. Perhaps you buy some stamps or stationery stores. Children can be bought something to eat like a banana or a fresh roll. They will soon understand that neither sweets nor crisps are on offer.

Make connections

- By your words and genuine interest, help the children to make links between what they see on different local outings. Perhaps you react to excited pointing from toddlers with, 'you're right! We know him. He's our milkman!'
- By about 18 months toddlers may start themselves to link local sights with images in some of their books or posters on the nursery wall. Be excited with them if they point out a picture of a squirrel, just like you all saw this morning.
- Make some of these links yourself in simple conversation with the children, when you share books or look together at posters and wall friezes.

From Two to Three years of age

Development within the third year

From their second to their third birthdays, young children change remarkably as they extend their skills, interests and understanding of their personal world. They have a sense of themselves as individuals. Already you will see the difference between young children who have been encouraged and those who have experienced far too much criticism or pressure in their lives.

Young children bring their previous experience to bear on the present and their expectations will shape how they approach play materials or react to new adults. Young children are egocentric in that they cannot easily look beyond their own perspective. There is much about the world that they do not yet understand but older twos and young threes become more aware of what they do not know. 'Egocentric' does not mean self-centred in a negative way. On the contrary, within a warm emotional environment, young children do sometimes consider others and show concern for the feelings of peers.

Children's physical skills, both large and fine movements enable them to move around and explore. They find out more about how everyday objects work and experience pleasure in their sheer ability to run, jump, climb and play vigorously with their friends. Their skills, and understanding of sequence around familiar events, make young children genuinely helpful within the daily routine. Having a trusted part to play supports their confidence and self esteem.

The ability of young children to use language extends into a broader use of their communication skills as well as an impressive vocabulary. Children's mistakes tend to be logical, based in what they know so far and often very sensible guesses beyond that boundary. They show creative uses of language and developing rich pretend play. What children say, the logical mistakes that they often make and the evidence of their imagination remind adults just how much even these young children are already thinking and reasoning.

Physical or learning disabilities will shape the pattern of young children's development, as will persistent ill health. The responsibility of caring adults is to ensure that disabled children are enabled to play and be part of daily routines, along with appropriate adjustments and realistic expectations in line with the specific disability.

Developing relationships

Early communication

Developmental focus

Young children now use many more words and combine them into meaningful and original phrases and then short sentences. Their mistakes in word combinations or basic grammar are usually logical. By the end of the year, children use their language in different ways: asking questions and telling you about events. They work to express feelings or simple ideas and, with adult encouragement and a good model, twos and young threes are increasingly able to think out loud. Some children will be learning two languages and can become bilingual speakers successfully.

Children's understanding of what is said to them has expanded tremendously and they will have learned a range of strategies for communicating that they do not understand you or need more information. Depending on their experience, young children can be learning the social skills of communication, about listening and trying not to interrupt.

Will you help?

■ Ask children for their opinion when choices can be made, like how best to display their models.
■ If a small group of children come up with several possibilities, then involve them in the plan to order the choices, for instance, the stories they would like to be read this afternoon. 'So, first we'll have.. then we'll...'
■ Involve them in tasks that need some thought or planning. It might be: 'I can't find the thick paper. Where do you think we put that away?'
■ Or the suggestion could be, 'let's go to the baker's this afternoon. What shall we buy for a treat for tea...what will we need to take with us on the trip?' This kind of suggestion moves naturally into writing a list and some twos will be keen to 'write' their own – a good example of really early literacy in action and reasons for writing.

I wonder what, whether, how....?

■ Encourage children to use their words to speculate and wonder. They are able to increase their vocabulary of

Pause for thought

The EYFS, along with the curriculum frameworks around the UK, highlights the great importance of encouraging young skills of communication. Young children need rich early experiences of personal, ordinary exchanges. The EYFS stresses the theme of Positive Relationships, because communication develops within the welcoming atmosphere of a genuine, personal relationship between caring adults and young children.

The ideas in this section, as elsewhere in the book, are reminders of how much simple conversation matters. Children take their lead from familiar adults. How you behave sets a good example about showing interest, listening and waiting rather than interrupting. The key is to talk with children, not at them, and to listen as much as you talk. Sometimes you start the conversation, but make sure that you also follow children's lead, listen to what interests them, the questions they want to ask you.

For under threes this communicative exchange is between no more than two or three individuals. Under threes cannot communicate within group sessions – such activities come across as too impersonal and the waiting time to speak is too long. However, practitioners need to be very cautious about weighting communication towards group times for over threes.

words that support their thinking out loud.
■ With a familiar or a new book, ask the children, before you turn the page, 'ooh, what's going to happen now?' or 'how will he get out of this mess?'
■ Use daily opportunities to involve children in considering a range of possibilities, like, 'our tomato plants are so tall they keep falling over. What could we do?' or 'I wonder what'll happen when we add the water to this mixture?'
■ Personal care routines are easy opportunities to support the kind of wondering that is 'maybe I need to...' Young children can be encouraged to think 'I am hot, I'll take off my jumper', or 'it is cold outside so I need my jacket'.
■ If a child has been outside and stepped in puddles, they can be encouraged to think 'I need dry socks'. If they have forgotten to roll up sleeves or are wet, then they may need to change a piece of clothing.

Do you remember when...?

- Young children love to reminisce about shared past experiences. It may be something exciting, puzzling or just a happy time.
- It can be fun to relive experiences through words or maybe photographs as well.
- Follow children's lead when they want to talk about the fire engine you all saw yesterday or the dead baby bird that you buried in the garden last week.
- Share your memories as appropriate. Perhaps you smile and say, 'I was remembering when I stepped in that big puddle and you all laughed so hard'.
- Some nurseries use this practical idea to help sharing recent memories. Young children, with their agreement, have a sticky label on their clothes that always starts with, 'ask me about...' and then something special about today. It might be 'the big spider' or 'our trip to the market'. Parents know to ask and practitioners can help with vocabulary if a two-year-old gets stuck. The same system can work just as well for sharing events from home.

Having a good natter

- Children will enjoy talking with each other. Value their conversations, listen in sometimes and avoid interrupting them.
- Look to create quiet areas inside and in the garden where friends, or you and the children, can simply sit and chat.
- Make sure that you sometimes ask children questions when you do not know the answer, so they can have the pleasure of telling and explaining.
- Do some 'research' by looking at a child's favourite book or television programme so you understand what she wants to share with you.
- Talk with parents so you can know who are the potentially bilingual children in your setting. Speak the language in which you are most fluent, but it would be friendly to learn some words in the child's home language.

Social development — making friends

Developmental focus

Within this age range, young children who have been supported in a sense of their own self-worth are more able to behave in ways that adults recognise as social. However, they are still very young and we owe them the

Pause for thought
Children vary in their developmental pattern but sound knowledge of child development is necessary in order to identify when individuals are now delayed.
Familiar carers should understand most of what older twos say. It would be a source of concern if a three year old were incomprehensible to a parent or familiar carer. In the same way, children should show that they understand simple language from familiar adults and children. They still use all the clues of the situation and predictable routines, but children should now understand the words.

respect of realistic expectations, rather than demanding actions in areas like 'sharing' just because it makes life easier for us as adults. You will help children far more if you assign some thinking time to realising just what you are asking if you say, 'take turns' or 'think about other people sometimes'.

Young children need help in group life for a wider range of social skills than adults usually recognise. By all means watch and see if children can manage but be ready to help where necessary. Young children may need your support to join a group that has already begun a play activity. One child may need a sympathetic ear to deal with the distress of being rejected by a group, yet another may need support to make some distance from another child who clings closely than the first child wishes.

Getting along together

- Look carefully at the organisation of your setting or how you arrange children's social life with home-based care. Children cannot get to know each other if they rarely encounter the same children. Very flexible times for a crèche or nursery may suit the adults, but can disrupt the predictability that enables children to make friends.
- Watch, listen and let the children themselves show you who are their close playmates. Help young children to relate well together by creating an environment in which they do not have to compete over play materials or adult attention.
- Look carefully at your day and re-organise times when young children have to wait so long that squabbles are more likely or boredom begins.
- In group care, look for ways to make drinks and nutritious snacks easily available (the self service snack bar), rather than part of a long-drawn out snack time during which young children can get understandably cranky. A few children will often then make a real choice of 'let's have our drinks together now'.

Pause for thought

The EYFS has a strong emphasis on sound knowledge of child development, with the understanding that such knowledge must guide practitioners in creating a day that is a good fit for young children. They like a predictable routine but, within that familiarity, children do not benefit from over-organisation of their play experiences.

It is especially important that social situations are small-scale and intimate - that means flexibility and responsiveness to what twos fancy doing now. They want you to sing with them when they ask for a song or rhyme. Or to enjoy this book right now, not for it to be put aside for a later group story time.

Early social skills

■ Thank children for their help or ideas and encourage them to tell others about the activity with 'we found these pieces' or 'do you want some of our gingerbread?'

■ Promote the idea of timed turns by using a large sand timer or a mechanical egg timer. Children who experience fairness are more likely to show it in return.

■ Set a good example to the children by showing you have noticed what they managed. Offer warm remarks such as, 'I do like that!' or 'well done, you were so careful with the rabbit'. Listen and you will hear children use similar remarks to each other.

■ Help to make snack or meal time a pleasant time of company and conversation as well as eating. Show a good example yourself of courtesy, sharing and turn taking at snack time. Encourage appropriate language by asking around the table 'Rebecca, would you like one? or 'Dai, could you please pass me…?'

Are you feeling ….?

■ Children may have the words for many familiar objects, people and actions but expressing feelings is more complex. Watch them and listen to what they say, so that your suggestions can be sensible as well as tentative. It might be, 'Harry, you look a bit sad. Are you sad about something?' or 'Angie, are you cross about the collage? I know, it's very annoying when you've worked hard and things won't go right.'

■ Listen to children within conversation and don't tell children what they feel or that they 'ought not' to feel something. You would not appreciate somebody telling you in this way and nor do children.

■ Read stories that explore feelings of individual characters: happy excitement, social troubles or missing someone. A puppet or cuddly may also be the main character in a story that you tell which raises the idea of feelings and 'what shall he do?' Enjoy the story and talk a little about the people – keep it simple.

Co-operative games

■ Look for activities on which children can work together, with your support. Keep the groups very small otherwise the waiting overcomes the interest.

■ Plan a craft activity in which the separate steps are straightforward, although the end result can be impressive. Young children – if they wish - can work together on patchwork designs in paper, card or material.

■ Simple cooking and food preparation can enable young children to take turns, watch each other and use their abilities towards a joint project which is then shared at eating time.

■ Indoor or outdoor gardening can draw on young children's physical skills and encourage co-operative activity in digging, planting and watering.

■ Use books that repeating story lines for young children to chime in together or to take turns to supply the phrase.

■ Sometimes make photo books or scrapbooks to record and celebrate joint activities. Parents will be interested but the children too will enjoy looking back over 'what we all did'.

Using the senses

Seeing, exploring and understanding

Developmental focus

Young children can see what you see, assuming nobody has visual disabilities, but they cannot yet make sense of everything. Young children are building up their experience of the world and this includes visual information about qualities of objects such as shapes, size or colour. They need broad opportunities to use their vision in everyday activities, then they will in time be ready to assign the words to these qualities. They are best helped by adults who comment appropriately on what they and the child can see. You 'drop' words into the conversation about 'big', 'green', 'round' or 'high up' and children can link your words to what they see. In time they will use this vocabulary in their own speech.

Young children's ability to concentrate will steadily extend when they are encouraged and enabled to look carefully and to scan for detail. They enjoy this focussed play and involvement in ordinary daily tasks. Sometimes they just enjoy looking at interesting or new sights. Involved adults can encourage children's willingness to stop and stare and sometimes to be enchanted.

Busy pictures

- Get books or posters with large pictures of familiar scenes or events. Encourage children to look at the pictures, scanning the details in a relaxed way.

Pause for thought

The EYFS places great importance on considered organisation of the learning environment for young children – outdoors as well as indoors. A clear system for storing materials and equipment, helps children to put away as well as get out items. They can look and check, as well as remember where the cars, jigsaws or tools are kept. Labelling storage areas or containers with simple pictures, as well as a written label, helps children to look carefully and to take care of their environment.

- Ask them to choose their favourite part of the picture and to talk about it if they wish. You can invite in an open-ended way such as, 'Tell me about the…' or 'what's going on in that corner?'
- Play search-and-find by asking the children to spot objects, animals or people in a book or a poster picture. Begin with easy and familiar items, then try a few more difficult suggestions.
- If children are intrigued by this spotting game, hold up an item and ask the children to find it in the picture. Make some collections of items that link with a given picture.

Copy me

- Stand in front of the children and get them to face you. While demonstrating and naming actions, encourage the children to copy you. For example, touch the floor, jump up and wiggle your nose.
- Get the children to suggest actions and you copy them.
- Develop this idea by introducing the children to 'Simon Says'. Feel free to change it to your own name. And introduce children to action songs where they have to use hand-eye co-ordination, such as 'Head, shoulders, knees and toes' and 'if you're happy and you know it, clap your hands'.

Can you find it?

- Make two sets of ten cards with pictures of everyday items that can be found in the nursery and are easily accessible.

- Place one set of cards in a bright attractive bag and invite the children to explore its contents.
- Ask questions like 'what have we got here?' to ensure that each child can identify the items on the cards. Draw their attention to the cards, one at a time, then ask them to find the real item in the room.
- Talk about the pictures with the children. You might comment on the item itself, the colour, shape or size and where the real item is kept in your room (but not all in one long exchange!)
- Get the children to place the item and the card next to one another.
- Develop this activity by placing the second set of cards around the room - on the walls, chairs, table, sink and so on. Hold up a card and ask the children to find its matching partner. Alternatively, shuffle both sets of cards, turn them upside down on the floor, get each child to pick a card and let the others take turns to find its partner.
- Or play 'I spy' with qualities that young children will recognise, for instance, 'I spy with my little eye something that is very fluffy' or 'something that goes "squeak!"'
- Take photos of local features outdoors such as the nursery's sign, a local shop and a telephone kiosk. Give the children some of the photos, take them on a walk and ask them to look for the items in their photos. Help them as much as they wish. Alternatively, use photos of natural items such as fir cones, leaves and twigs.

Touch and feel

Developmental focus

Young children now have a well-developed and sensitive use of touch. This sense is combined with good abilities to look, grasp and manipulate small and larger objects. They learn from a wide experience of appropriate hands-on experience of play materials and ordinary objects. Children have some understanding of unpleasant touch, things that are too hot or that hurt or scrape them. They are still learning about common dangers and need adults' patience and guidance to continue to understand so that they can increasingly take good care of themselves.

Friendly touch as contact, communication and comfort is still important and children may use touch to comfort a friend. They will appreciate your close contact so long as you respect individual preferences in how young children want to be comforted and do not demand cuddles as an adult right.

Socks off!

- Help children to take off their shoes and socks. Join in barefoot yourself.
- Sit on the floor with the children and wriggle your toes about.
- Try feeling different objects with just the feet; children can close their eyes and try to guess if they want. Try a banana, potato or other familiar fruit and vegetables. Feel a book, a teddy, paper tissues or building bricks.
- Try to pick up objects with both feet or the toes. It is not easy, so emphasise the fun in trying.
- Walk on different textured surfaces: some lino, a piece of deep pile carpet, some textured wallpaper, a rectangle of foam or the wadding used in quilting, a roll of cotton wool and popper wrap. Introduce words like 'soft', 'rough', 'scratchy' or 'slippery'.
- Put bare feet in the sand pit or a bowl of soft sand. Wriggle your toes in the sand, bury your own or a child's feet and watch the toes break free.

Different strokes

- Make a feely book with the children. Have a wide range of materials and sort them out by feel.
- Encourage the children to stroke and touch the materials and help them with the words to describe what they feel. Soft feels from silk and velvet, flower petals, feathers or cotton wool. Rough textures from velcro, some leaves or a flat scourer. Shiny material from flattened milk bottle tops or lengths of ribbon.
- Some materials may be hard to describe: a bath sponge may be rough or squishy, knitting wool may be fluffy or a bit scratchy.
- Stick the materials into a scrap book, letting the children make their own choices from the available materials.
- Choose some books about touch and the other senses to read to children. One example is the *Touch and Feel* series (Dorling Kindersley).

Eyes closed

- Take some familiar objects and toys and put them into a large cloth bag or a cardboard box with a lid.
- Children put a hand into the bag or box, feel for an object and try to guess what it is before bringing it out to see.
- Encourage children to feel carefully before guessing and help them with the words to describe what they can feel.
- Join in the game yourself and make a couple of deliberate mistakes, especially if the children find it hard to guess.

Heavy and light

- Feel a feather on one hand and a toy car on the other. Show children how to weigh up each side. Try with other objects which vary in weight.
- Have two bags, ideally ones you can see through, and explore how it feels when different objects are put into each bag and they are lifted, one in each hand. Experiment with different amounts of the same objects in each bag, for instance, building bricks or spoons.
- Introduce the words of heavy and light and look for opportunities in the day to add to the children's understanding. Perhaps you might say, 'all these books are too heavy for me' and look as if you are struggling a bit. Then ask, 'can you help me? Can you carry one book?'

Smelling and learning

Developmental focus

Young children have a well-developed sense of smell and some clear preferences about 'nice' and 'horrid' smells, just like their views on tastes. It is useful for adults to remember that a good sense of smell can help to keep us safe and healthy, for example, by alerting us to food that is going bad or to the danger of fire.

Children can learn more about the range of smells and link appropriate words to the scents when they are offered a rich variety of learning experiences that provide access to new as well as familiar smells. They will extend their language by describing the smells they like and dislike, those they don't mind and those that remind them of certain occasions or places. See the Pause for Thought on page 12, because those comments still apply here.

Cooking smells

- Alert children to the smells of food and cooking. Comment on the smells of ingredients when you do simple cooking with children.
- You can place jelly in warm water, watch it melt and smell it. Include a variety of essences in baking activities.
- Suggest that when cooking at home, parents allow their child to smell the rich and varied scents of the food they use, as well as any herbs, spices or sauces that are added to flavour the foods.

Bathroom and washing smells

- Have pleasant-smelling soaps to encourage the children to wash their hands. Alert them to the scent of other toiletries, either that you have in the nursery bathroom or that you naturally wear.
- Young children may start to recognise familiar toiletries such as perfume, deodorant, bubble bath, shaving foam, soap, toothpaste or aftershave. Make the links with parents to scents in the home.
- In the nursery and through links to children's homes, draw children's attention to the scents of washing powder, fabric conditioner and washing up liquid. Use any natural opportunities to confirm that some cleaning substances are not for children, only for adults to use.
- Put different scents, for example, peppermint or lemon essence, soap flakes or bubble bath, into play dough and water.

Perfumed pictures

- Collect scented crayons, pens or pencils, paper, ordinary crayons and a brightly-coloured bag.
- Give each child a blank sheet of paper and encourage her to use ordinary crayons to make marks on the paper. Invite children to smell the picture.
- Now put the smelly crayons in the bag, ask what they think you have in it, and suggest that it is something that can make their pictures have a scent.
- Ask each child to take out one of the crayons. In a low voice stress how special they are. Invite them to smell one of the special crayons then an ordinary one, and ask, 'Are they different?'.
- Invite children to use the special crayons to draw a picture and then smell it.
- If children are interested ,then extend this activity by using each crayon separately. Invite the children to smell each colour once and guess the smell.

Smelly soaps

- Place four to six bars of fruit-scented soap, wrapped in some netting, inside a large decorative bag. Ask the children to take them out one at a time and invite them to identify the smell. Bear in mind that some scented soaps are closer to their supposed smell than others.
- Encourage them to pass the soap on to the next child and to describe it if they wish, by shape, colour, smell or any other quality.
- Ask children's for their opinions, do they like the scent or not, which is their favourite?
- Cover the soap with cotton material, then ask the children to identify just by smell, having taken away the colour that sometimes gives a visual clue.
- Allow the children to wash their hands with their favourite bar.

What's that smell?

- Place a variety of items, such as grated chocolate, orange peel, sliced banana, sherbet, peppermint cream, grated cheese and jelly cubes, into small bowls or containers.
- Ask the children to take time to smell each one. Then blindfold one child, offer her an item and invite her to guess which it is. Repeat with the other children.
- While the children are blindfolded, introduce a new item to challenge their smell ability – tell them 'This is a new smell'.
- They can taste some items after they have identified them.

Hearing and listening

Developmental focus

By this age young children are able to name many sounds and match them to their source. Children can be encouraged to develop their powers of auditory discrimination when you incorporate sound into everyday activities in the nursery and you alert children to sounds within the daily routine. Young children's ability to concentrate is a combination of looking and listening. So activities that help them to listen and make sound deliberately can support their growing ability to focus.

Young children are interested in a range of activities that involve rhythm, basic movement and exploration of beat. They can learn how to tune into sounds as well as a sense of achievement in making the kinds of sounds and

patterns that they want to create for themselves. Use of percussion instruments can combine sound and feel since they produce vibrations that children can experience as well as creating the actual sounds.

Hearing the sounds

- Set a good example to the young children by listening yourself and following their suggestion to hear an interesting or intriguing sound.
- Use an instrument or a bell as a listening focus: to call children's attention or to signal part of the routine, such as time to tidy up or that lunch is coming.
- Play a range of games to identify recognisable sounds, including sound lotto.
- Repeat a rhyme several times, then leave out the rhyming word and let the children fill in the missing word.

Getting it on tape

- Show children a microphone and tape recorder and tell them that you will record their voices. Ask the children to say a rhyme, one at a time or in pairs. Record and play it back. Children may initially be dubious that this is indeed their voice.
- Use a pre-recorded tape of sounds around the home, such as a tap running, telephone ringing, door bell ringing, toilet flushing, children laughing, car starting and car horn beeping.
- Ask the children what they hear and then ask if they would like to make a tape. Take them outside to identify noises they want to tape, such as children playing, dogs barking, a 'green man' beeping or a fire engine siren.
- Let each child record a sound then return to a quiet area to listen to the recording.

Pause for thought
Similar issues and concerns still apply as were raised on page 34.

- Keep the communication open with parents and have a full conversation with families whose disabled child joins your setting.
- Encourage parents to obtain medical checks, where appropriate since difficulties in vision or hearing, however slight, will complicate the learning task for young children and delay appropriate help.

Noisy trays

- Fill trays with a large amount of items, such as pasta, rice, cotton wool balls, marbles and tin foil. Watch that the children do not put small items into their nose or mouth.
- Place the trays on the floor and give each child a beanbag. Ask them to drop the beanbag on to the tray and then to describe the noise.
- Let them play with the bean bags and trays as they wish. You could suggest that they use hands and feet to make a noise in the tray.
- As a follow-up, place the trays in an open box, so the children can throw the bean bags into them. Before they throw the bags, ask them, 'will it be noisy? What do you think?'

Strumming

- Let the children look at a guitar and ask them what they think will happen if you touch the strings. Some children may recognise the instrument if someone at home plays the guitar.
- Let children touch the strings. Strum and pick the strings, making notes yourself and then allow the children to experiment.
- Repeat the experience with a violin or other stringed instrument.
- Talk about the hole in each instrument. Then offer the tissue boxes and elastic bands, and ask if they can suggest a way to make their own guitar.
- Let the children attempt to do this, giving help when asked. Have a little concert if the children want to.

Language and creative development

The young child as artist

Developmental focus

Young children who are given a range of materials can be fascinated by their ability to create beautiful images, unusual designs and new textures. At this age, children are unlikely to set out with the intention of drawing anything specific, although nearly threes may start to tell you that their painting is of a person or particular object.

Creative activities give children pleasure and satisfaction and provide a positive focus for their physical skills and visual abilities. They will still enjoying painting with hands and fingers but can also manage chunky brushes and other tools. Young children benefit from having a range of colours and textures from which to choose. They need the chance to experiment rather than copying examples made by adults.

Using the tools

- Experiment to find the size of brush or other tools that individual children can best manage.
- The simple approach is often best. For example, give children buckets of water and large paintbrushes or small rollers (from DIY shops) and allow them to 'paint' an outdoor wall.
- Large feathers, shower scrunchies, plastic cars (to be washed afterwards by the children, ideally) – there is a wide variety of possible, simple tools for young children.
- Hands, fingers and feet (shoes and socks off) remain excellent tools for large scale painting projects.
- Let two-year olds practise using scissors. They will be safe if you remain close and you can then help them. Children often appreciate someone holding the paper firmly while they cut. Allow the children to snip thin, pre-cut lengths of paper.

Rub along

- Make rubbings by placing paper against textured surfaces and help children to create an image by rubbing with a wax crayon. Use coins, leaves, paper taped to the bark of a tree or anything suitable with a raised surface. Encourage children to feel the surface before they rub. Rubbing works well with paper laid on asphalt, if your outdoor area has some of this surfacing.
- Make a patchwork collage with ready-cut shapes of different material or textured paper and wallpaper. Encourage children to stroke the materials as well as create a patchwork of their own choosing.

Printing

- Printing allows children to create attractive and interesting patterns quickly and easily. You can make paint thicker by adding a little flour. Encourage children to experiment with a range of printing techniques -
- Natural items can be used, such as shells, leaves, flowers, sliced fruit - orange, apple, star fruit and vegetables - peppers, carrots, onions. Cut shapes into halved potatoes and show the children how to paint and print.
- Or try combs, corrugated card, cotton reels, sponges, keys and toothbrushes.
- For screen printing, roll a sponge over a doily or other patterned item.
- Fold some paper in half and open it up again. Dip some string into the paint, making sure it all gets covered. Put the string on to one half of the paper and fold the other side of the paper on top of it. Press down hard all over, then open. For a different effect put something heavy on top of the folded piece of paper and slowly pull out the string.

Display with pride!

- It is always children's final choice about whether they want their production on display. But look for different ways, with children, to show what they have made.

- Take photos – and increasingly offer if the child would like to take the photo. Twos and young threes may well be ready for a series of photos that tells the story of 'how we made a big.....'
- Discuss with children how they would like any images or 3-dimensional models laid out. Keep what you write to a minimum and let the children's choices speak for themselves.
- Have a regular shelf for displaying today's great works. Consider also a shelf where children can safely put their 'works in progress' away.
- Create 'art behind the curtain' with an attractive curtain that can be pulled back to reveal a painting or a shelf with models. With the children's help, regularly change what is behind the curtain.

Enjoying and making music

Developmental focus

Young children can enjoy making and listening to music. They practise their physical skills and use their communication in music making, singing and listening. They will move to rhythms, make sounds with toys and instruments, sing, chant and listen to a variety of forms of music. Singing with children is an effective way to support their language skills and vocabulary. Young children often sing spontaneously as they go about their day-to-day play activities. They enjoy experimenting with instruments and the sounds they create. Never insist that young children perform in front of a group. Invite everyone as individuals but neither press, nor label the less enthusiastic ones as 'shy'. Let them go public in their own time.

Live music and singing performances are a source of interest for many children, either to perform themselves or listen and watch others. Children's horizons can be extended if you invite parents or other local people who sing or play instruments to come and share their talents in the nursery.

Sing-along

- Gather a repertoire of songs and rhymes as these will help develop the children's awareness of the sounds that make up the beginnings and ends of words in the language. Such awareness supports early literacy.
- In a similar way, gather songs and rhymes that help early numeracy skills. For example, 'Five Little Speckled Frogs' and 'Ten Green Bottles'.
- Make routines more interesting by making up songs to go along with the actions, for example, 'This is the way we wash our hands' or 'This is the way we brush our teeth' to the tune of 'Here we go round the mulberry bush'
- Starting to play a familiar music tape or a CD is a useful way to let children know it is time to tidy up or to gather for story time.

Music corner

- Set up an area in the nursery where children can experiment with different basic instruments.
- Place the instruments in storage boxes where the children can easily access them. Label the boxes with pictures of the instruments so that they can easily return them to the correct box.

- Allow the children to experiment with them freely. Be ready to spend time yourself with the items until children are familiar and start to initiate their own use of the sound makers.
- Sometimes tape the sounds the children create and play them back. Invite the children to point to the instruments as they hear them being played on the tape.

Simple sound makers

- Collect lidded containers such as film roll canisters, vitamin containers (so long as you can peel off the label to give a blank surface) or margarine tubs.
- Fill two of each container with materials that create a noise when shaken, for example, rice, sand, glitter and pennies. Use these as percussion instruments to accompany songs.
- Your store of filled plastic bottles (see page 10) will also be effective sound makers for little hands.

Pause for thought

Of course it is important that children become able to read and write, when they are developmentally ready. The developmental materials for under threes in the EYFS focus strongly on how skills of really early literacy are built through experiences. Good stories for young children unfold with a recognisable rhythm and this experience helps children to tune into sounds and sound patterns as they occur in everyday speech. This phonological awareness, that needs to be offered within the shared activity and without any pressure on the child, will help them a great deal when they are finally ready to read.

Repetition within a story and having favourite stories many times helps children to anticipate, recall and join in as they wish. This experience supports their language and thinking skills. An early pleasure in books, the stories and the illustrations, is an invaluable support to children's later literacy. They need the sense of enjoyment just as much as their growing awareness of how books and print work.

This section is an appropriate time to remind readers in England that the EYFS Early Learning Goals apply to the end of the stage: the reception class year. The ELGs on reading, writing and handwriting are irrelevant to under threes; practitioners should look at the suggestions under the younger age ranges. It is also necessary to state that a considerable number of early years specialists, including the authors of this book, challenge these specific goals as developmentally unrealistic for 'most children' by the end of the EYFS, which is the working definition of any ELG.

Pick a song

- Young children may now know enough songs to make specific request but you can encourage an active choice.
- Collect props that are part of the story told in a nursery or rhyme. Or create a simple image from a song and laminate the picture. Put these items into a cloth bag and let individual children pick one item, without seeing, from the bag. Let them guess the song or rhyme and then sing it together. Then the next child makes a lucky song dip.

Sound story

- When children become familiar with songs and stories they can be made more interactive by adding sounds.
- For example, for 'Goldilocks and the Three Bears', one child can be given wooden blocks or a pair of shoes to tap on the floor for Goldilocks' feet. An empty bowl and spoon can be used for testing the porridge. When the beds are being tried, one child could pat a pillow or cushion. When the bears come back, three instruments can be used to represent each of the bears, for example, a drum for daddy bear, a tambourine for mummy and maracas for baby.
- Breaking the story into parts and listening to the sounds helps develop children's ability to listen and their awareness of the sounds instruments make.

Dancing time

- Young children enjoy simply dancing along to familiar music. Join in and don't be self-conscious; young children will never criticise your dance style.
- Make a collection of old silk or cotton neck scarves. You can ask parents to donate or buy cheap ones from charity shops. Select a piece of taped music and take the children to a large clear space indoors or outdoors. Play the music and get the children to dance to the music with a scarf in each hand.
- The dance time works well also with long, wide ribbons. You can offer children instructions and model different actions. For example, wave your ribbons up in the air, wave them quickly, wiggle the scarf behind your back.

Tell me a story

Developmental focus

Stories are an important part of the day for young children because listening to different kinds of stories supports children's all round development. Stories can be enjoyed through books read out loud by an adult, but stories are also part of oral story telling without a book, songs, poems and rhymes. Stories are also personal – what happened today.

Telling or reading a story to this age group should still be a personal time. Children approaching three years are more able to manage a group story time, but they will continue to enjoy and really need the close attention of being with an adult and only one or two other children. Spontaneous enjoyment of 'tell me a story' is the opportunity to return to this child's favourites or to look pleased at her choice. Your reaction supports her emotional development and sense of self esteem.

Personal stories

- Telling a story is about a narrative, a sequence of linked events. You will have some good stories in books for the under threes, but also look for the pleasure in personal and shared experiences within the nursery.
- Retell with the children the story of 'what we did today…' or 'what we saw in the market...' When children have especially enjoyed a local outing or seen an exciting sight for them, they often like to recall the experience as a personal story.
- Follow the children's lead and always try to respond if they ask you to re-tell their story with key reminder requests like 'talk about the big puddle' or 'say the pussy cat story'.
- Involve the children as much as they want with starters such as, 'Once upon a time, Jane went to the park with…..' (and invite the names of the children), followed by 'and then what happened was…..' and 'but what did we see then? It was…'
- Re-tell favourite shared experiences in a very similar format each time, so that children can join in easily if they want.
- Perhaps children notice and become fond of a bird or animal that visits your setting. Try making up some stories about what 'Robbie Robin' or 'Henrietta Hedgehog' might be doing during the day or night when you do not see it.

Making storybooks

- Sometimes you can make the book of the personal story for children. Create a simple scrapbook or a sequence of photos in a self seal album.
- Be ready to tell the story to the children or help them as they tell parts of what happened, pointing to the illustrations.
- See if the children want to illustrate your stories of the nursery hamster or the visiting wild creature.

Different story tellers

- Support a tale or a story poem with a puppet or suitable soft toy. See what the children like the most and be creative in how you share the story with your fellow story teller.
- The teddy or hand puppet may be the main story teller. You do not need to be a ventriloquist. If Teddy is well to the fore and makes movements, then the children happily suspend disbelief and accept that he is telling the story, even though you are saying the words. If you can do a slightly different voice, then that helps, but the main point is to tell a good tale.
- Some tales work well with you as the main story teller and a finger puppet or two who comment on, interrupt or even argue over the events of the story.
- Some stories, from books or with linked television series, may have the main characters available as soft toys or puppets. Some children may like to tell a part of a recent episode through the toy. You can take a positive approach to the fact that many children do watch a lot of television and help them to make connections in this active story telling role.

Story poems and rhymes

- Good stories in the oral tradition (for adults as well as children) are often close to being poems.
- Look for some story poems, for instance, modern writers such as Michael Rosen or examples from previous generations such as A.A.Milne.
- You can tell the story poems with expression and the rhythm helps children to chime in, especially with repeating phrases. Add some suitable gestures and children will join in those as well.
- Children enjoy it when you pause before a key phrase or gesture and then deliver it, often with their loud addition.

Physical development

On the move

Developmental focus

Young children are now well co-ordinated and physically strong - compared with themselves as a baby or toddler. They are able to catch balls that are thrown directly into their arms, to stand on one foot, to stand and walk on tiptoe and to make other more controlled movements. Children have sheer pleasure in practising and applying their skills in play and lively games. They also need and enjoy space and playmates just for the joy of running about their environment. Your support for children's physical skills, and the importance of healthy exercise, can all be incorporated into your days, with and without additional equipment.

Some young children are more confident than others and careful support can encourage less bold children to extend their skills at their own pace. Young children need a safe enough environment and adults who help to keep them from harm. However, they also need challenges and opportunities to begin to assess for themselves the element of risk: 'how high do I go?' or 'how do we stop banging into each other?'

Get moving

- Encourage the children to start playing movement games, such as tag, musical chairs and ring around the roses. So long as you are active in the game, it is very likely that children will want to play.
- Children of this age can be introduced to skipping ropes, bean bags, quoits and hoops to encourage physical activity.
- Encourage the children to become more deliberate and controlled in their large movements. Show them movements and invite them to copy.
- They could jump up and down and land with feet together and then with feet apart, or land with left foot forward, then land with right foot forward. Stand facing a child, holding each other's hands, and then slowly lean to one side lifting the other leg off the ground, then swap legs. You will have more confident balance than twos, so be ready to wobble a bit yourself and not look too 'good' at this game.

- Have a resource of games for playing outside. Young children still like '1,2,3 go', hide and seek and run-and-chase. But they can also be ready for simple outdoors music and movement or following you around the garden in a weaving 'snake' line.
- Use the garden to encourage children to use their growing physical skills. Create a basic route for steering their trikes and push along vehicles.

Physical challenge and fun

- Create an obstacle course – indoors or outside. You could include: an old box to climb through, large pillows to climb over, a fabric tunnel to crawl through, hoops to step through, a board to walk across, cones to run in and out of, a short, low slide with a mat or ring at the bottom and balls to roll. Let children experience with their whole body what it means to go under, round, through and over the top of the items of equipment you have used – and get involved yourself.
- Ask the local builders' yard for spare pallets. Sand them down to remove any rough edges and/or cover each one with tough, non-slip material. Stepping or jumping off a pallet can feel adventurous to a young two year old. Some also like to use the pallet as a simple 'stage'.
- Ask around (friendly builders' yard again) for guttering and milk crates (friendly milk delivery service) and make these available outdoors. Show children how they could build with this equipment and establish any necessary ground rules – probably the limit to how many crates are piled up together.

Walking the line or Giant's footsteps

- Collect thick catalogues or old phone books – all of the same thickness – and cover with textured paper (to stop slipping). You could draw on the outline of an enormous, giant's foot or patterns. Involve the children and see what they would like.
- Suggest the children go barefoot (again to reduce slipping) and place the blocks in a line with narrow gaps in between. Let the children explore 'walking the line'.
- Then see – today and another day – if they would like to try the blocks/feet a little bit further apart, so they have to stretch,

- Try a zigzag line or pretend they are stepping stones across a rive – 'watch out for the crocodiles!'

Musical games

- Put on a tape or CD with lively, happy music. Move in different ways and encourage the children to copy you.
- Try some of these: wave your arms, nod your head, sway back and forth, stamp your feet, rock from side to side, shake your hands, clap your hands. Follow some of the children's own ideas for movements.
- Sit on the floor with a child and face each other in a straddle position, or as close as you can get and hold hands. You form a rough triangle shape. Lean forwards and encourage the child to lean back, then alternate. Sing a variety of songs while doing this - for example, 'Row, Row, Row your Boat' or 'See-Saw, Margery Daw'.
- Use a variation of playing with scarves to music. Tie a single scarf onto a hair scrunchy and make a generous number of these pairs. Invite children to put one scrunchy on their own wrist, and take one yourself. Explore moving the scarf to music and add another scrunchy for the other wrist if children would like.

Pause for thought

Physical development is one of the six areas of learning established in the Early Years Foundation Stage. Exploration and fun with physical skills is just as important as any of the other five broad areas. This message is valuable in itself, since young children's enthusiasm for learning as a whole can be dampened if they are required to be physically inactive.

However, an equally important point is that of the holistic nature of young learning. Try any of the suggested activities in this section or the following one. Observe closely what children are happy to do in imitation of an enthusiastic adult, but also how they begin to make the game their very own. What do you think they are learning? In what ways are they exploring and extending their current skills? We are confident that you will notice developments in several, maybe all, of the other broad areas of learning.

Using fine physical skills

Developmental focus

Young children now have an impressive array of fine physical skills and these support them in their wish to become more independent in daily life. For example, young children will be able to manage many of the tasks involved in feeding themselves and drinking. They will be able to use everyday implements like a spoon or to eat fairly neatly with their fingers. Around familiar settings they will be able to turn a knob to open a door, unscrew lids or pull out the container they want for their play. They are far more able now to manage fine movements required in order to turn the pages of a book one at a time and to handle the fastenings and more tricky parts of dressing and undressing themselves.

The development of fine physical skills takes time and practice. Adults at home or in the nursery owe children patience and understanding as two and three year olds attempt to master the skills that depend on finger and thumb co-ordination, and linking vision with physical skills and planning. Children with physical disabilities may need some further help or soon appreciate specialised implements. However, within this additional support, disabled children will want to apply and extend their skills just like their friends.

Doing it myself

- Build up children's confidence by introducing them to more challenging play materials as they are ready. This age range will be more able to handle jigsaws with several pieces and smaller construction material.
- Support children's confidence by offering help as they wish and creating enough difficulty and novelty to interest but not to daunt children.

- To help the development of children's fine motor skills and aid their growing independence, provide cups and eating utensils that are small enough to fit their hands.
- Place tissues and paper towels where children can reach them easily. Place coat hooks at the children's height; provide individually marked toothbrushes for each child and place them in an accessible location.
- Encourage children to hang up their own paintings to dry on a string 'clothesline' using clothes pegs.

In and out, on and off

- Collect generous amounts of basic, safe resources and let children play with them in their own creative ways. This could be lots of cardboard tubes and scarves – may be threaded, tied, laid out – watch and see what children do.
- Have wooden mug trees and kitchen towel holders and a set of materials that could be hung or pulled over these items – large wooden curtain rings or hair scrunchies. See what children do with these resources and take some photos to remind you of young creativity when children are allowed to explore.
- Make a collection of buttons – larger sizes – and stay close by, because twos will most likely try to put them into their mouth. Gently dissuade children from this action and model looking at the buttons, sorting them in any way and using little containers.
- Have an assortment of small containers: plastic food containers, washed out margarine boxes, little metal bowls (like the balti bowls that can often be bought in Pound Shops) or measuring cups.
- Collect the plastic trays from supermarkets that hold yoghurts and the like. Provide these trays with containers of dry pasta, large buttons and beads. Let children pour and sort as they wish.
- Collect any little set of drawers (Pound Shops sometimes have cheap ones) and unwanted holders for notepads. Again offer these with a range of items that can be organised by children.

Fill it up!

- Get an empty wine box carrier that has separate compartments. Give the children empty plastic water bottles. Encourage them to fill up the box by placing an empty bottle in each compartment.
- When the children have mastered this task with empty bottles, fill the bottles up with coloured water (tap water and food colouring) and let them continue with the task in hand.
- In the bath or beside a bowl of water, give the children some empty bottles. Encourage them to unscrew the top and use the lids as a pouring vessel to fill the bottles.

Work for little fingers

- Give the children who are fairly confident in using crayons a new experience by taping either sandpaper, a piece of plastic net, a square of carpet or corrugated card to a table top. Tape large sheets of paper on top and allow the children to make marks. This will encourage them to hold their crayons firmly.
- Gather pencil sharpenings, sequins, petals, small pieces of wool and string. Show the children how it is possible to make a simple mosaics and let them explore the materials. (As with the buttons, dissuade children from putting these items in their mouth.)
- Set up simple weaving activities by providing a large resource of ribbons, scarves, wool and other items that can be threaded in and out. Set up a secure wooden trellis, or fix large hole garden netting over a hula hoop, or over a plastic washing basket. You could also get a large piece of large hole rug canvas and, ideally, fix it securely to a wooden frame.

Using the environment

Getting outside

Developmental focus

Most children are now confidently mobile to reach whatever part of your garden or yard they wish to explore. They still have a limited grasp of risk and outdoors hygiene. So, your role is to continue to offer friendly supervision and a close eye on hand washing after some activities, especially any kind of gardening.

The children are ready and keen to extend their vocabulary: learning more words about what they see and do in the garden, to talk about the activities and to reminisce with you later. The outdoors may be some children's favourite place to look, listen and use their senses. Young children who enjoy the outdoors will be ready to extend their interests with simple, illustrated reference books and they may then spot, out in the garden, what they previously saw in a favourite picture book. They make connections.

Green fingers

- Do some planting with the children. Help them to learn about digging or making a small hole, patting down the plant, bulb or seedling and waiting for it to grow.
- If you have limited growing space, then invest in pots, window boxes or grow bags. (Using only clean earth or compost will be especially important if cats or dogs get into your garden, or you work in a part of the country where tetanus is a serious risk for gardeners.)
- Provide some small watering cans for children to sprinkle their plants or any other parts of the garden, especially during a hot spell.
- Talk with the children about the plants, flowers and grasses as they appear. Share their delight as the shoots start to push through the earth. Try to grow some vegetables or fruits that can be eaten later in the year.

Taking the indoors outside

- Unless the weather is really harsh, take play materials outside, such as the sand and water tray, painting easels or construction materials on an outdoor table. Make sure everyone has appropriate clothing for the time of year and invest in simple shelters for your outdoor space.
- Let children take part in the nursery domestic routine. Set up an outdoor activity of washing the dolls' clothes or other small play materials. Talk about what you are doing and introduce relevant words like 'wet' and 'dry'.
- Have drinks or snacks outside and let the children enjoy the experience of eating al fresco in their own 'café'. Perhaps one or two would like to 'take the orders' and then serve the 'customers'.

Pavement art

- If you have a paved area, you can encourage the children to be pavement artists with plenty of coloured chalks.
- You can mark out a roadway for the children's play with small cars or for a route they follow on the trikes and push or pull along vehicles.
- Chalk some large shapes with the children and play stepping into and out of, or walking along a wide line.
- Make an area of the yard damp with water and let the children make wet footprints out and away over the dry area.
- Experiment with painting with water on a dry surface using big brushes. On a hot day, watch together,

perhaps counting, how long it takes for their drawing to dry and vanish.

Let's pretend

- Young children love large boxes, so make sure there are enough for all. The boxes may now be cars, boats, fire engines, as well as homes or castles.
- Build hideaways and camps with the children by throwing a large sheet or blanket over the climbing frame or putting up a small tent in the garden. Let them bring out a selection of pretend play material from the home corner to equip their den.
- Take some photos of the activities so that you can all enjoy them later as you remember together.

Let's do weather

- Keep track of the weather each day. Let the children look carefully out of the window and then go out into the garden. Find the right picture and get a written label to fix onto your weather board. Introduce them to words about warm, cold or windy and to talking about sunshine, rain or clouds.
- Wrap children up warm to enjoy a fall of snow in the garden. Let them enjoy the delight of making footsteps in the fresh snow.
- Use an umbrella and get out in light rain. If the downpour is heavy, then watch the rain from indoors and when it has slowed, or stopped, go outside. Explore where the water has gathered, where it goes down the drains and how much it has filled up any containers in the garden.

Garden creatures

- Help children to learn the names of the creatures they see in the garden: squirrels, spiders, butterflies and perhaps a toad if you are lucky.
- Help children to build their general knowledge by looking with them for pictures in their books of similar creatures, or flowers and trees.
- Take some photographs of the wildlife in the garden and of the plants at different times of the year. Make a photo book and use this resource to help children recall what you all saw or their earlier gardening exploits.

Bringing the outdoors inside

- If you are waiting for the weather to be more welcoming, try some indoor gardening. Grow sprouting carrot or pineapple tops on a window shelf. Some herbs grow well indoors.

- Grow mustard and cress on damp blotting paper or cotton and eat some when it is ready. But be aware that not all children like the taste.
- Pick some flowers, leaves or twigs and create a simple arrangement with the children. Change the display from time to time.
- Get some green florists' block, which enables you and the children to push in twigs, or flowers with a strong stem.
- Cover a small board with reflective paper to make an unusual display base. Children may also enjoy making a pretend pond with this base.

Watery ideas

- Look around the nursery and your local environment for interesting sources of water. There may be a local common or park with a pond or stream that children can enjoy, so long as they are safely supervised.
- Watch the ducks on the water, landing and taking off. Twigs and leaves may travel along the flow. Look for a quiet place for children to drop stones into the water and see the ripples that this creates.
- When the sunlight is right, children may see themselves reflected in the water. Perhaps you can disturb the image with a stick and then wait for it to settle.

- A local gardening centre may have little fountains or artificial water systems and sometimes tanks of tropical fish that can enchant children.
- Explore natural water sources with weather watching. With the children, watch the rain run down the windows and off the roof. Draw in the condensation if it forms on the panes.
- Collect some rainwater in a container and see how high up it reaches.
- Ensure all children are equipped with wellington boots, then they can enjoy walking through puddles.
- In very cold weather, show children how the water sources in the garden have frozen. Put out water that will freeze over night and then bring in the container and see how long it takes to melt in the warm indoors. Do the same activity with a container full of snow. Use words to describe temperature like 'freezing', 'cold' and 'getting warmer'.

Travelling and learning

Developmental focus

Young children are ready to be delighted by what seem like very ordinary outings to adults. What is obvious or even boring to you is experienced as new by young children. Local trips can be a rich source of learning so long as the adults view any trip through the eyes of the children. What do the children find interesting? When do they want to stop and stare? What is a sensible timing for the children? You may well organise some special trips during the year, but young children appreciate all the local trips that cost no money or very little.

Young children are now able to recall some of your previous outings, to talk about what you will do and later

Pause for thought

Young children need authentic experiences to feed into their pretend play and ordinary, local outings are perfect 'raw' material. You will then hear and see how twos and young threes extend these events within their imaginative play.

Children can see what actually happens in the train station or bank. Young children also enjoy collecting leaflets and forms that can be placed in the pretend post office area. Involve children in the selection of any shopping and give one or two children the chance each time to hand over the money. They will begin to understand how buying, paying and getting change works.

what you have seen on the trip. They will be able to walk all of a short trip, although their limited understanding of safety means they must be carefully supervised all the time.

Getting involved

- Talk with children about today's trip before you start. Make them feel involved in the plans.
- Help the children to think ahead with descriptions like, 'first we'll go to the library and get some new books. Then shall we come back past the road works? We can see if that big hole is still there.'
- Manage children's expectations for when it will soon be time to go. Perhaps you can say, 'one more chase around the bushes, then we need to pack up'.

Reminiscing

- While you are on the trip, talk with the children about what you all see and hear. Listen carefully to what they want to say and look at what they want to call to your attention.
- Encourage children to talk about local trips to colleagues when you return to nursery or to share interesting events with parents. Do not press children, but encourage them in any wish to share memories.
- Consider taking a camera to record special events and listen to children's views on what is worthy of a photo. A record of the burst water main in the main road may be just as important and exciting as the baby goslings.
- Sometimes make a display of the photos or any drawings that children wish to make. Collections of interest to the children like conkers, autumn coloured leaves or unusual rocks can make a special display.

Changes over time

- Support children's ability to recall other outings with return trips to locations where there will be continuous change.
- Plan a series of trips to watch the baby ducks, or other animals you see regularly, as they grow.
- Return to watch how the chestnut blossom has produced conkers or the sycamore 'helicopters' have spiralled to the ground.
- Even gardens will have flowers that mature and perhaps vegetables like tomatoes or green beans that children can notice as they grow.
- Urban environments can generate interest in children. Return to watch the changes as the road has been dug up and gradually re-laid or the new block of flats that is steadily being built.

Learning from travel

- Young children can safely become more active in your outings through involvement in their choice of routes. They will start the process of learning to be independent local travellers.
- Offer one or two children the chance to be 'trip navigator' and let them guide the group on the familiar route to the library or the market. Help the navigators if they are uncertain and ensure that the role is enjoyable.
- Help the group to anticipate routes and landmarks with, 'now what do you think we'll see just round this corner?.... Yes, it's the fire station! Let's see if the fire engines are there.'
- Take all the practical opportunities to show children how you keep them safe on the roads. Say out loud what you are doing on their behalf and help them to be a safe part. You might say, 'let's find the crossing', 'That's the red person so we wait.... now here's the green person so we walk across'. If there is no pedestrian crossing, then alert children to how you look and listen and judge the safe place and time to cross.
- Many children now travel mainly by car, so look for possibilities to take a short bus or train trip. The enjoyment is in the ride itself as well as showing children how to travel in this way, buy tickets and plan a journey. You may alight the other end and walk a little, but a circular trip will be just as much fun. Watch out for the sights and the interest of seeing familiar landmarks from a different angle.

Suggestions for further reading

National guidance materials are usually free as hard copies to practitioners working in the relevant part of the UK. However, most resources are now on the internet, so are easily available to all interested childcare professionals.

The Early Years Foundation Stage materials can be ordered from DCSF Publications tel: 0845 60 222 60 - reference number 00012-2007PCK-EN. Materials can also be downloaded from these two websites: www.teachernet.gov.uk/teachingandlearning/EYFS or www.standards.dfes.gov.uk/EYFS

Birth to Three: Supporting Our Youngest Children can be ordered from Learning and Teaching Scotland telephone 0141 337 5000, but many resources can be downloaded from www.LTScotland.org.uk/earlyyearsmatters

These materials are also useful for supporting good practice with the under threes.

- *Creating Places for Birth to Threes* (Community Playthings) Tel: 0800 387 457 www.communityplaythings.co.uk
- Dorman, Helen and Dorman, Clive *The Social Toddler: Promoting Positive Behaviour* (The Children's Project 2002) www.childrensproject.co.uk
- *Learning Together* series (Early Education). Leaflets are free or can be downloaded - tel 020 7539 5400 www.early-education.org.uk
- Featherstone, Sally (ed) 2007 *L is for Sheep: Getting Ready for Phonics* (Featherstone Education Ltd) www.featherstone.uk.com
- Featherstone, Sally (ed) *Like Bees, Not Butterflies – Child-Initiated Learning in the Early Years* (Featherstone Education Ltd 2008)
- Healy, Jane *Your Child's Growing Mind: Brain Development from Birth to Adolescence* (Broadway Books 2004)
- Hughes, Anita *Developing Play for the Under 3s: The Treasure Basket and Heuristic Play* (David Fulton 2006)
- Lindon, Jennie *Understanding Children's Play* (Nelson Thornes 2001)
- Lindon Jennie *Understanding Child Development: – Linking Theory and Practice* (Hodder Arnold 2005)
- Lindon, Jennie *Helping Babies and Toddlers Learn: A Guide to Good Practice with under Threes* (National Children's Bureau 2006)
- Lindon, Jennie *Care and Caring Matter: Young Children Learning through Care* (Early Education 2006)
- Lindon, Jennie *What Does It Mean to be Two? (Revised Edition)* and *What Does It Mean to be Three? (Revised Edition)* (Step Forward Publishing 2008)

- Trevarthen, Colwyn et al *Meeting the Needs of Children from Birth to Three* 2003 summary on www.scotland.gov.uk/2003/06/17458/22696 report www.scotland.gov.uk/Topics/Research/Research/14478/9218

Videos/DVDs

- Dowling, Marion *Supporting Young Children's Sustained Shared Thinking: An Exploration* (Early Education 2005) and *Exploring Young Children's Thinking Through Their Self-Chosen Activities* (Early Education 2007)
- Goldschmied, Elinor *Infants at Work: Babies of 6-9 months Exploring Everyday Objects* (Revised Edition) (National Children's Bureau) 020 7843 6000
- Goldschmied, Elinor and Hughes, Anita *Heuristic Play with Objects: Children of 12-20 months Exploring Everyday Objects* (National Children's Bureau 1992)
- *Birth to Three Matters: A Framework to Support Children in their Earliest Years* (Sure Start 2002). The framework will be replaced by the EYFS, but the good practice shown in this visual material has not been replaced.
- *The Value of Unit Block Play* (Community Playthings 2000) 0800 387 457
- *Baby It's You: The First Three Years* 1994 (includes an extra programme about brain development) (Woodside Promotions 1994) tel: 01372 805000
- *The High/Scope Approach for Under threes* (High/Scope UK 1999) tel: 0870 777 7680
- *Tuning Into Children* (National Children's Bureau 1997)
- *Life at Two* (2007) and *The Wonder Year* (Siren Film and Video Ltd 2008)tel: 0191 232 7900 www.sirenfilms.co.uk
- *The Social Baby* (2004) and *The Social Toddler* (The Children's Project 2005) tel: 020 8546 8750 www.childrensproject.co.uk